LOCOMOTION PAPERS

AF088970

THE PONTYPRIDD, CAERPHILLY & NEWPORT RAILWAY

by

Colin Chapman

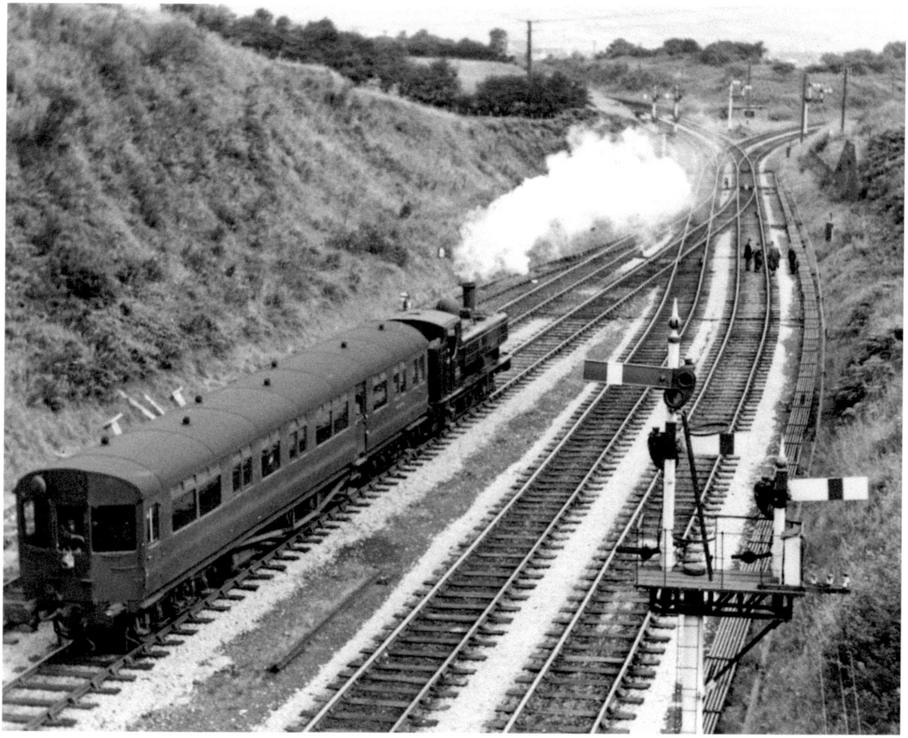

A train leaving the Pontypridd, Caerphilly and Newport line at Penrhos Junction on its way to Newport. *S. Rickard collection*

THE OAKWOOD PRESS

© Colin Chapman, 2003

ISBN 978-0-85361-771-6

First Published in the United Kingdom, 2024.

Printed by
Claro Print, 1 Spiersbridge Way, Thornliebank, Glasgow, G46 8NG

Publisher's Note: Colin Chapman was the author of several books on railways in South Wales. He died in 2009 leaving this manuscript unpublished. It was passed to the Welsh Railways Research Circle who contacted Oakwood Press to publish it, his last book.

Alexandra (Newport & South Wales) Docks & Railway Locomotive No. 22 was purchased from the Mersey Railway in 1905. As their No. 6 *Fox* it had been used on Mersey Tunnel services which required the condensing apparatus to reduce the amount of steam escaping into the confines of the tunnel. *Author's collection*

Front cover: A single coach auto-train, hauled by No. 6411, arrives at Nantgarw Halt on 4th September, 1956. The notice of withdrawal of the passenger train service has been posted on the end wall of the up side shelter. *S Rickard collection*

Back cover: A view from above of PC&N Junction on 13th May, 1952, with the former PC&NR line bearing away from the ex-TVR main line to the other side of the Taff Valley. The class '56XX' 0-6-2T is standing at the site of Tramroad station, while in the distance are the Interchange Sidings, then used for wagon storage. *R. C. Riley*

Published by
The Oakwood Press, 54-58 Mill Square, Catrine, KA5 6RD
01290 551122   www.stenlake.co.uk

Contents

Preface		5
One	Introduction	5
Two	Background and Early Schemes	7
Three	Promotion and Construction	29
Four	Open to Traffic	47
Five	Under the Alexandra (Newport & South Wales) Docks & Railway	73
Six	Grouping to Closure	89
Seven	Along the Lines	101
Eight	Locomotive and Train Working	133
Nine	Postscript	157
Index		160

Approaching the junction with the former Rhymney line at Penrhos, a Pontypridd–Machen auto-train speeds under the three arch bridge near the junction. *D. K. Jones*

Preface

Prior to the enlargement of the Great Western Railway at the Grouping in 1922 South Wales was a veritable hornet's nest of fiercely independent local railway companies. One such company was the Alexandra (Newport and South Wales) Docks & Railway (AD&R). As its name suggests the AD&R Co. was primarily a docks concern, but the company also owned about 7½ miles of 'main line' railway. The lines in question had originally belonged to an independent company – the Pontypridd, Caerphilly & Newport Railway (PC&NR) – albeit one which had extremely strong links with the docks company. Together with the use of the privately owned Tredegar Park Mile Railway (TPMR) and running powers over parts of the Rhymney and Brecon & Merthyr Railways, they provided the PC&NR and its successors with a through route from a junction with the Taff Vale Railway (TVR) at Pontypridd to the Alexandra Docks at Newport.

This study focuses on the history of the PC&NR rather than that of the Alexandra Docks. Having said that, and given the close relationship between the two, it would not be possible to deal adequately with the PC&NR without also referring to the development of the docks and the interaction between them and our subject railway. Although this perspective has determined the approach adopted here, it is freely acknowledged that the complete story of the Alexandra Docks merits a detailed study in its own right.

The PC&NR formed but part of the through route between Pontypridd and Newport. Of the other lines involved, one – the Machen Loop Line – had been built by the PC&NR before being transferred to the Brecon & Merthyr Railway (B&MR). The Caerphilly-Machen branch of the B&MR saw relatively little traffic apart from that of the PC&NR. Between Bassaleg and Alexandra Docks the line through Tredegar Park, although remaining privately owned until after the Grouping, was effectively part of the PC&NR. For the sake of completeness, therefore, it has also been necessary to cover the history of those sections in other ownership in some detail.

Chapter One

Introduction

By the mid-1860s the railway network of east Glamorgan and the western part of Monmouthshire was already well developed. The first stage of this process had seen the ports of Cardiff and Newport linked with their respective hinterlands, the railways concerned making use of the natural routeways provided by the main river valleys. The River Taff provided a direct run from Merthyr to the sea at Cardiff for the Taff Vale Railway, cutting through the range of hills forming the 'southern crop' of the coalfield basin at Taff's Well. The River Rhymney, on the other hand, after following a parallel route as far as Caerphilly, then veered eastwards towards Newport, its path blocked by Caerphilly Mountain. It then turned to the south at Machen, before making its way round the higher ground and eventually reaching the sea at Pengam, to the east of Cardiff. No railway was ever to follow the river's circuitous course to the south of Caerphilly. However, to the east of Machen, a gap at Rhiwderin, near Bassaleg, provided a potential outlet from the Rhymney Valley through to Newport, while a break in the hills to the west of Caerphilly

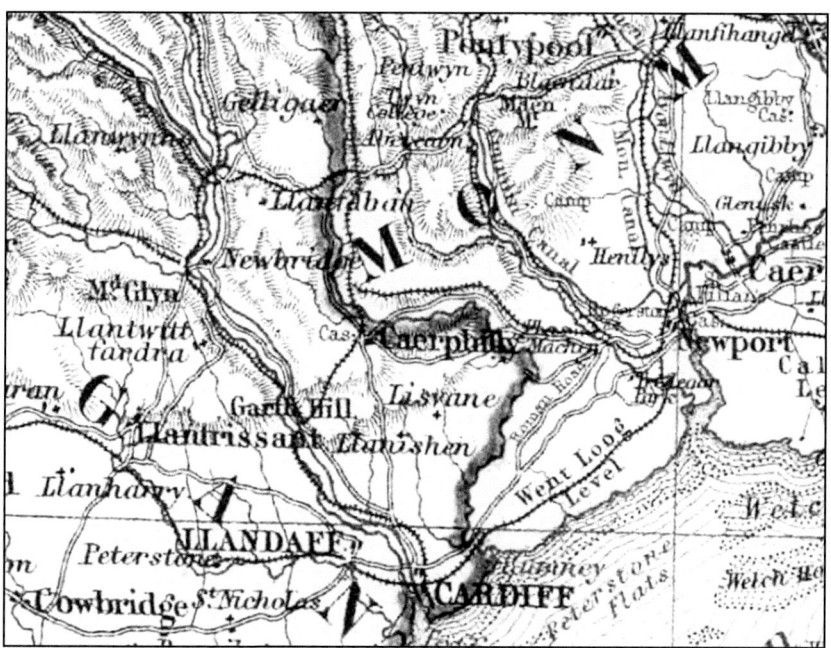

1860s map showing railway development near the Glamorgan-Monmouthshire boundary.

gave an alternative, although steeply-graded, prospect of reaching Cardiff via the Taff Valley. As a result, the Rhymney Valley was always to have divided loyalties, with the early Rumney Railway (and its successor the Brecon & Merthyr Railway) taking the former route in its approach to Newport, and the later Rhymney Railway making use of the latter (initially at least) to get to Cardiff. To the east, Newport provided the natural focus for the tramroads (later railways) of the Sirhowy Tramroad and the Monmouthshire Canal Co., via the valleys of the Sirhowy and the Ebbw.

Strong east-west routes had also been developed. The South Wales Railway, opened between Chepstow and Swansea in 1850, had, in true Brunelian fashion, avoided the higher ground altogether by following the coastal plain between Newport and Cardiff before utilising the broad valley of the River Ely, to the west of Cardiff. In complete contrast, the Taff Vale Extension of the Newport, Abergavenny & Hereford Railway (opened throughout in 1858) and the Merthyr, Tredegar & Abergavenny Railway (opened with extensions between 1862 and 1879) had both struck out, in spectacular fashion, against the grain of the country, forging links between respectively Pontypool Road and the TVR at Quakers Yard (and from 1864 Neath, via Aberdare and the Vale of Neath Railway), Abergavenny, Dowlais and Merthyr.

The remainder of the 19th century and the years up to the outbreak of the First World War witnessed an ever more complex pattern emerging as a result of intense competitive pressures. This third stage of development saw the growth of new and expanded outlets for the export coal trade, together with the emergence of a complex web of competing railways linking the various ports to the different parts of the coalfield. As a result, a number of these later lines forsook the narrow confines of the main river valleys to exploit various side valleys, gaps and other more or less helpful physical features in their pursuit of viable alignments to reach their objectives. The subject of this study is one such line, which was promoted and built to connect the Taff Vale Railway at Pontypridd with the Alexandra Dock at Newport, passing from the valley of the River Taff via those of the Rhymney and the Ebbw in the process.

Chapter Two

Background and Early Schemes

As the Pontypridd Caerphilly & Newport Railway was intended to provide a direct link between the Taff Vale Railway and the Alexandra Dock at Newport, while taking advantage of as much of the existing railway network as possible, it will be helpful to give a brief outline of the history of the various components of that network, together with the development of the Alexandra Dock, up to the promotion of the new railway company in 1877.

Monmouthshire Railway

Rail transport came early to Newport, albeit in the somewhat primitive form of a 4 ft 2 in. gauge plateway, worked by horses. In particular, the Monmouthshire Canal Act of 26th June, 1802 provided for the construction of the following tramroads:

- The Sirhowy Tramroad, from Tredegar to Nine Mile Point, near Risca, with branches;
- From Nine Mile Point to the canal and River Usk at Newport (with a branch to Crumlin), to be built by the Monmouthshire Canal Co., with the exception of about a mile through Tredegar Park;
- The 'Tredegar Park Mile', to be made and maintained by its owner, Sir Charles Morgan I, with power to charge tolls for its use.

The route was opened throughout in 1805. According to the *Monmouthshire Merlin* of 26th December, 1829, the first steam engine ran over the tramroad on 17th of that month, but lost its chimney on contact with an overhanging tree in Tredegar Park! The tramroad was subsequently extended from Risca to Ebbw Vale and Nantyglo, the Newport-Ebbw Vale/Nantyglo route in time becoming known as the 'Western Valleys Line'.

By its Act of 31st July, 1845 the canal company was empowered to use locomotives and required to convert the tramroad to a 4 ft 8½ inches gauge railway, in line with the recommendation of the Gauge Commission, published that year. Sir Charles Morgan II came under a similar obligation to improve the Tredegar Park Mile Railway. Under a further Act of 14th August, 1848 the canal company changed its name to the 'Monmouthshire Railway and Canal (MR&C) Co.', the Act also providing for the carriage of passengers and the elimination of haulage by horses on its lines after 1st August, 1849. Faced with the need to

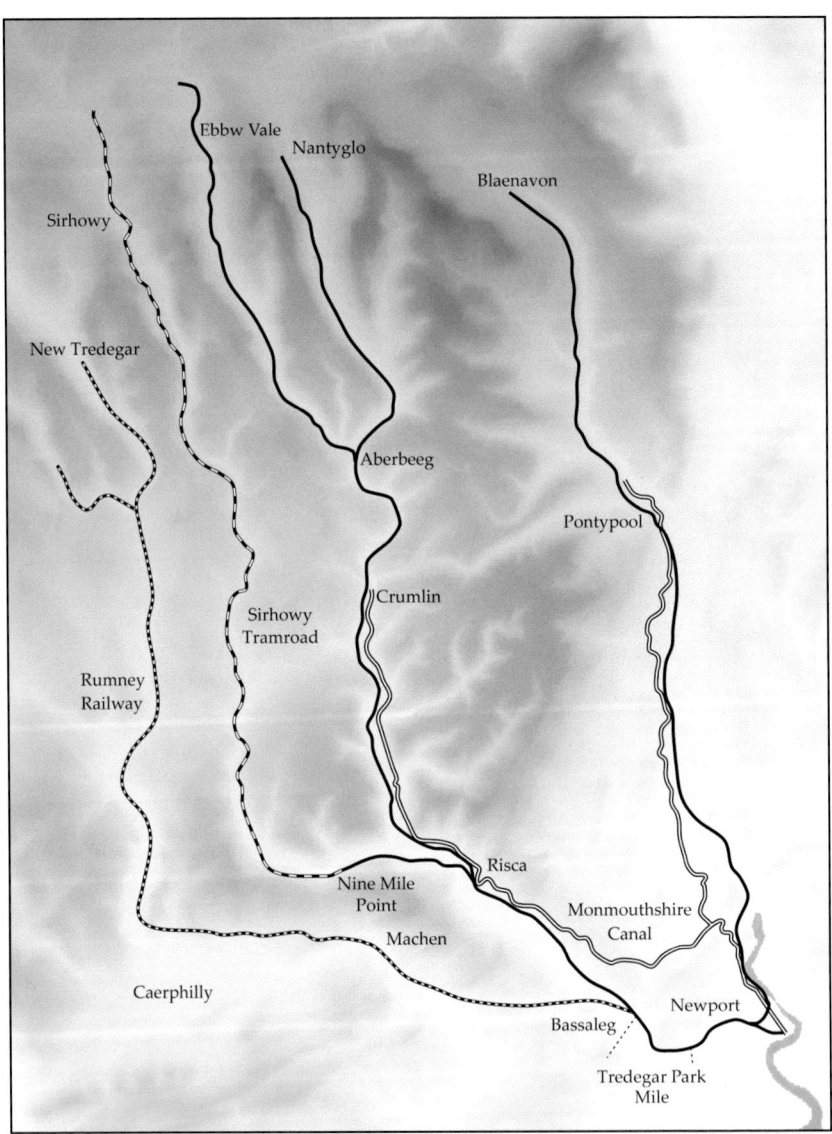

Map of the Monmouthshire Canal & Railway, the Sirhowy Tramway and Rumney Railway in the early 1850s.
Relief shading contains OS data © Crown copyright and database right 2024.

accommodate existing traffic and the requirement to convert to a standard gauge railway, the Monmouthshire Railway and Canal Co. adopted a combined railway/tramroad rail, and in this form the Western Valleys Line was opened to passenger traffic between a temporary terminus at Court-y-bella, on the outskirts of Newport, and Crumlin, together with a branch to Blaina, on 23rd December, 1850. The main line service was extended to Ebbw Vale on 19th April, 1852, and to Dock Street terminus in Newport on 4th August of that year. Conversion to a normal standard gauge railway followed, being completed by May 1855, with the exception of the branch from Risca to Nine Mile Point which had been so altered by the following November.

A connection, albeit in the form of a transfer station accessed by a backshunt from Waterloo Junction, was made between the Western Valleys Line and the broad gauge South Wales Railway in 1852. This link became a proper junction – Western Valleys Junction (Alexandra Dock Junction from 1882) – on the conversion of the South Wales main line to the standard gauge in May 1872.

The Sirhowy Tramroad (renamed the Sirhowy Railway by Act of 25th May, 1860) was also converted into a standard gauge railway, with a passenger service being introduced between Sirhowy and Newport (Dock Street) on 19th June, 1865. Under an agreement of 21st August, 1875 the Sirhowy Railway was acquired by the London & North Western Railway, this being confirmed by that company's Act of 13th July, 1876.

The Monmouthshire Railway & Canal Co. was leased to the Great Western Railway for 99 years on 1st August, 1875, with full amalgamation following on 1st August, 1880. In 1874 the Monmouthshire Co. had obtained parliamentary powers for a deviation of its line in the vicinity of the Cardiff Road crossing to the west of Newport, together with a connecting spur from this line to join the South Wales main line. A revised scheme, authorised in 1876, retained the deviation line, but provided for a new route for the connection to the main line. This link – from Park Junction to Gaer Junction – was brought into use on 1st January, 1879, this being followed by the opening of the rebuilt and enlarged High Street station at Newport on 11th March, 1880. Western Valleys, Sirhowy Valley and Brecon & Merthyr Railway trains, all of which had previously used Dock Street station, were then diverted to the new main line station: those from the Western Valleys on 12th May, followed by Sirhowy Valley and Brecon & Merthyr Railway services on 1st June, the date of closure of Dock Street station.

Rumney Railway

The Rumney Railway, often referred to as the 'Old Rumney' to distinguish it from the later and decidedly more modern Rhymney Railway, was incorporated by Act of 20th May, 1825. It was built as a 4 ft 2 in. gauge plateway, worked by horses, from Pwll-y-Llaca (south of Rhymney) to a junction with the Nine Mile Point Tramroad of the MR&C Co. at Pye Corner, south of Bassaleg, and had been opened throughout by 1830. It followed a hillside route on the eastern side of the Rhymney Valley, turning eastwards above Caerphilly and passing through Bedwas and Machen towards Newport. In 1853 the Old Rumney was described (albeit in a rather less than disinterested source – the prospectus for the 'new' Rhymney Railway Company) as:

> ...an antiquated contrivance, which is traversed in common by locomotive engines, and by the public on foot, and in gigs, carriages and carts'.

The prospectus went on to note that mineral traffic was also worked by horses and that:

> ...the curves and gradients of this tramroad are so severe that a locomotive engine has difficulty in transporting from the Bristol Channel to the Rhymney Ironworks, a distance of only 21 miles, 30 tons of iron ore during a whole day.

By this date the original plateway had given way to a combined edge rail and tramplate track compatible with that used by the MR&C Co.

Under the Rumney Railway Act of 1st August, 1861 the company was re-incorporated, with powers to improve and straighten the line and adapt it for the conveyance of passengers. This Act also authorised the building of a branch line from Machen to Van, to the east of Caerphilly, where an end-on junction was to be made with the Caerphilly branch of the Rhymney Railway. We will return to look in more detail at the subsequent history of this branch later in this chapter.

In 1863 the Brecon & Merthyr Railway, anxious to extend its territory southwards, acquired the Old Rumney, this purchase being confirmed by the Rumney and Brecon & Merthyr Railways Act of 28th July of that year. The substantially-upgraded line was opened to passenger traffic between Pengam and Newport on 14th June, 1865, with intermediate stations at Maesycwmmer, Bedwas, Machen, Church Road, Rhiwderin, and Bassaleg. The service was extended from Pengam to Rhymney on 16th April, 1866, and to Dowlais Top on 1st September, 1868, thereby completing the link between Brecon and Newport.

Taff Vale Railway

The need for an efficient transport link between the iron-producing district around Merthyr and the sea at Cardiff led to the promotion of the Glamorganshire Canal, opened on 10th February, 1794. However, apart from the historic Merthyr (otherwise Penydarren) Tramroad between Merthyr and Navigation House (modern Abercynon) and a number of other tramroad feeders to the canal, the Taff Valley did not see any significant development of rail transport until the construction of the Taff Vale Railway, authorised by Act of 21st June, 1836, and opened between Cardiff and Navigation House on 8th October, 1840 and onward to Merthyr on 21st April, 1841.

Midway between Merthyr and Cardiff and served by the TVR was the settlement of Newbridge, renamed 'Pontypridd' in 1843 (although the railway company persisted with the old name until 1866). Pontypridd was to grow in importance as a market centre for the Rhondda and other nearby coalfield valleys, in line with their increasing output and populations. In railway terms, however, the town's main significance was as the focal point for coal traffic from the Cynon, Clydach, Rhondda and upper Taff Valleys passing to the docks at Cardiff and Penarth.

Rhymney Railway

By the mid-1850s the Old Rumney was already perceived as an anachronistic relic unsuited to the transport needs of the iron and coal industries. In November 1853, with the support of the Marquess of Bute (who owned Bute Docks in Cardiff and had a vested interest), plans were deposited for the Rhymney Railway, extending from the terminus of the Llancaiach branch of the Taff Vale Railway to Rhymney, with branches to join the Taff Vale Extension of the Newport, Abergavenny & Hereford Railway at Hengoed and up the Bargoed Rhymney Valley. The connection to the Taff Vale Railway was soon struck out, leaving the authorised lines of the Rhymney Railway Act of 24th July, 1854 confined to the section between Rhymney and the Newport, Abergavenny & Hereford Railway at Hengoed and the Bargoed Rhymney branch.

The ambition to reach Cardiff still persisted, however, and on 2nd July, 1855 a second Act was obtained authorising the continuation of the line from Hengoed down the western side of the Rhymney Valley and through the gap in the hills to the west of Caerphilly to a junction with the Taff Vale Railway at Walnut Tree Bridge, near Taff's Well. In addition, a detached branch line was to run from the Taff Vale Railway, just north of that company's Cardiff station, to the Bute East Dock.

The section of the Rhymney Railway from Rhymney to Hengoed (including the connection to the Newport, Abergavenny & Hereford Railway) was opened to goods and mineral traffic only on 28th December, 1857, the extension southwards to Walnut Tree Junction following on 25th February, 1858. A passenger service was introduced between Rhymney and Cardiff on 31st March, 1858, serving, amongst others, stations on the west side of Caerphilly and at Walnut Tree Bridge, immediately adjoining Walnut Tree Junction. The TVR opened its own Walnut Tree Junction station alongside the Rhymney station on 22nd June, 1863, coinciding with the closure of its nearby stations at Pentyrch and Taff's Well. It was renamed 'Walnut Tree Bridge' on 1st June, 1886 and 'Taff's Well' on 1st April, 1900.

The Rhymney Railway Act of 1855 had also included a short branch from the main line towards Caerphilly. On 8th July, 1856 the company's engineer, Joseph Cubitt (1811-1872), recommended that a new route be adopted to serve coal workings at Van, to the east of Caerphilly, in place of the authorised branch. This new line, which was to leave the Rhymney main line at Penrhos, to the west of Caerphilly, was sanctioned by Act of 10th August, 1857, this Act also permitting the abandonment of the earlier proposal. Instructions to proceed with the works were given on 8th February, 1859, the single track branch being completed by the end of that year.

Cardiff and Caerphilly

The extension of the Rhymney Railway from Hengoed to Walnut Tree Junction was a considerable improvement on the scheme as originally authorised, but the section below Caerphilly was soon perceived as somewhat indirect and unduly dependent on the Taff Vale Railway for the connection to Cardiff. Relations between the two companies quickly deteriorated and thoughts soon turned to the prospect of a more direct and independent route to the port.

Unsuccessful attempts were made to promote a direct line between Caerphilly and Cardiff in the Parliamentary Sessions of 1861 and 1863. Finally, in 1864, following a fiercely fought contest with the Brecon & Merthyr Railway (which had put forward a very similar proposal), the Rhymney Co.'s scheme proved victorious, its Act receiving the Royal Assent on 25th July of that year. The authorised railway was to leave the Rhymney main line, just north of the original Caerphilly station, and

BACKGROUND AND EARLY SCHEMES 13

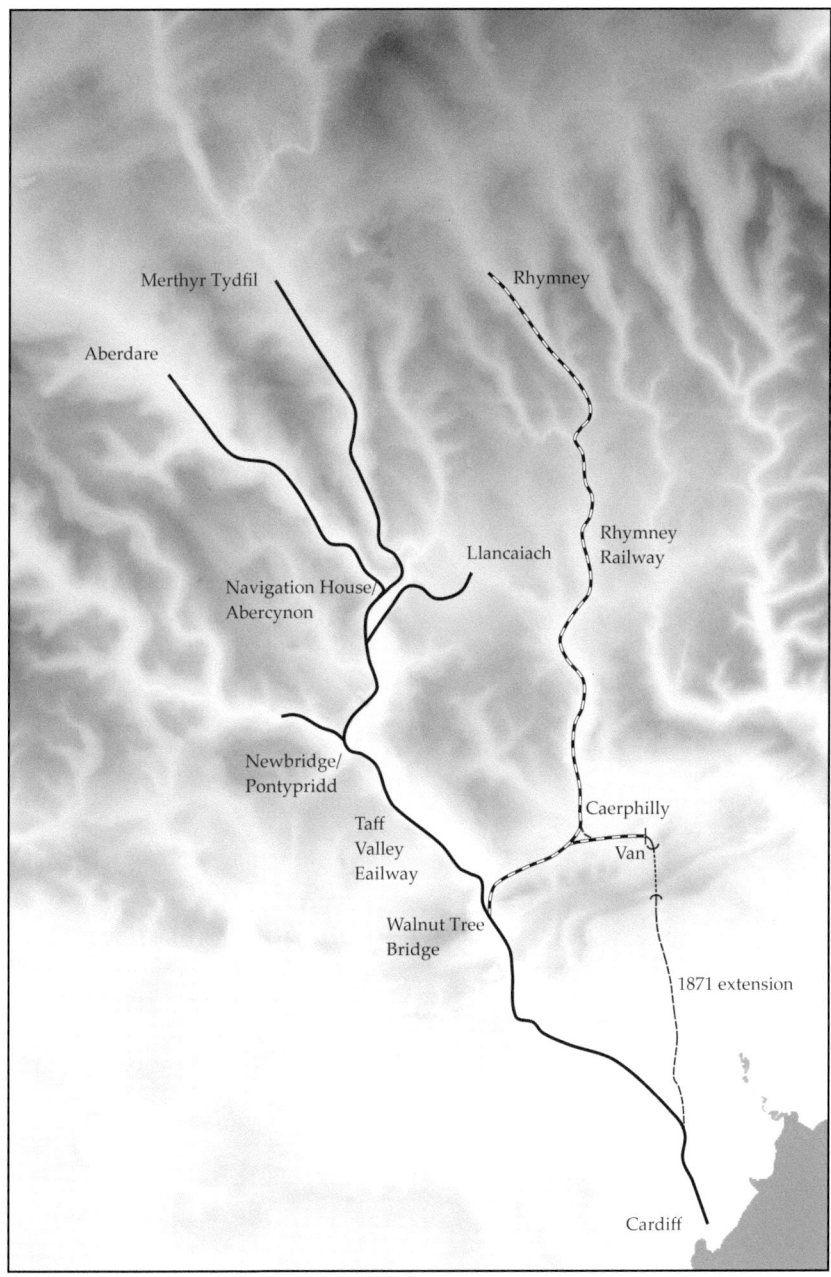

Map of the Rhymney and Taff Vale Railways about 1860.
Relief shading contains OS data © Crown copyright and database right 2023.

then turn to the east to join the company's Caerphilly branch. From Van, to the east of the town of Caerphilly, the new line was to branch off to the south, passing by a tunnel under Caerphilly Mountain, to join the Rhymney Co.'s East Bute Dock branch in Cardiff.

The Cardiff and Caerphilly line was opened to passengers and freight on 1st April, 1871, with a new station on the southern edge of Caerphilly on part of the old Caerphilly branch which had been incorporated in the new route. A residual passenger service was retained for a short time between Walnut Tree Bridge and the town.

Alexandra Dock

For much of the first half of the 19th century Newport was the chief coal exporting port in South Wales. Until 1831 it had enjoyed freedom from coal duties on traffic conducted to the east of the Holme Islands in the Bristol Channel. The repeal of this feature in that year was followed by the growth of intense competition between Newport and its main rival, Cardiff. In 1835 an Act was obtained for a new dock at Newport, the first sod being cut by John Owen, the town's mayor, on 1st December of that year. The 'Old Dock', as it was later known, was opened on 10th October, 1842, with an extension following on 2nd March, 1858.

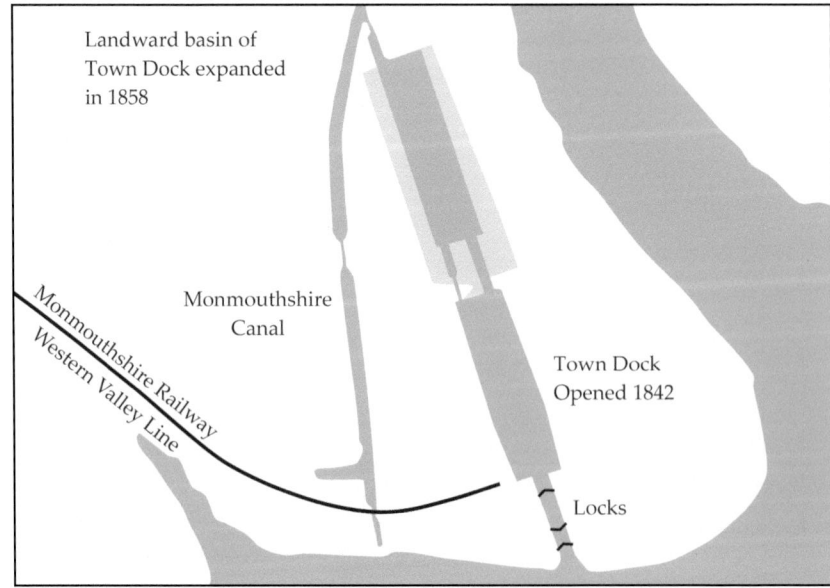

Sketch map of the Town (Old) Dock and its transport links in the early 1840s.

Cardiff's first dock, subsequently referred to as the 'West Dock', was opened on 9th October, 1839, with the larger East Dock being completed in stages between 1855 and 1859. As a result of these developments, Cardiff had, by 1865, expanded to a total dock area of 64½ acres, compared with Newport's 11¾ acres. Cardiff's dominance was also apparent in its export coal tonnage, which in 1865 amounted to 2½ million tons, against Newport's 900,000 tons, much of which was still accounted for by the old riverside wharves.

In the Spring of 1864 Alexander Bassett CE (1824-1887), engineer to the first Lord Tredegar, Charles Morgan III, put forward a scheme for a new dock on his Lordship's property on the west side of the River Usk, near its mouth. The Morgans had lived at Tredegar Park, to the west of Newport, since the early 15th century, the family's wealth having been considerably enhanced when John Morgan of Tredegar inherited valuable estates from his uncle John in 1715. In 1758 Sir Charles Gould (1726-1806) married Jane Morgan, acceding to the Morgan inheritance in 1792. Adopting the Morgan name, Sir Charles began to increase the family's fortune through various financial, industrial and commercial ventures. In particular, he promoted the establishment of coal mines and iron works, and was instrumental in the construction of the Monmouthshire and Brecknock & Abergavenny Canals. He also encouraged the building of the tramroad from Sirhowy to Newport. He was succeeded on his death in 1806 by his son, also Sir Charles (1760-1846), who built upon his father's success and was largely responsible for the early development of Newport as an industrial and commercial centre. A third Sir Charles (1792-1875) succeeded to the title in 1846, becoming the first Baron Tredegar in 1859.

Alexander Bassett was also, at this time, engineer of the impoverished Cowbridge Railway (opened in 1865) and was responsible for the promotion of a number of other schemes in South Wales. One proposal of particular relevance to this study was that involving a connecting spur from the Taff Vale Extension line, near Hengoed, to join the Brecon & Merthyr Railway below Maesycwmmer. This link, which was rejected by the Brecon & Merthyr Railway board on 13th September, 1871, was aimed at improving the route for coal traffic between Aberdare and Newport. Bassett was subsequently elected President of the South Wales Institute of Engineers.

Bassett's dock proposal was favourably received, and on his recommendation James Abernethy CE (1814-1896) was called in to report on the project, which he quickly blessed with his support. Abernethy had a wide-ranging career, including construction of the South Dock at Swansea in 1858. Between 1856 and 1860 he had undertaken his first work at Newport, involving the extension of the Town Dock together with the installation of hydraulic machinery for the shipment of coal. He was elected President of the Institution of Civil Engineers in 1880.

The dock project was taken forward by a group of promoters, including Lord Tredegar, ironmasters Crawshay Bailey of Nantyglo, Rowland Fothergill and William Foreman of Tredegar and John Lawrence of Cwmbran, together with Newport merchant George Jones and Thomas Brown of Hardwick House. On 21st December, 1864 the other promoters entered into an agreement with Lord Tredegar for the lease of 200 acres of his Lordship's land for the construction of the new dock. This agreement was confirmed by Lord Tredegar's Estate Act of 5th July, 1865. Bassett assumed the role of 'Acting Engineer', with Abernethy as 'Engineer-in-Chief'.

Plans for the new dock and its connecting railways were prepared for deposit in November 1864 for the 1865 Parliamentary Session. The Alexandra (Newport) Dock Act received the Royal Assent on 6th July, 1865, the intended dock being named after Princess Alexandra of Denmark, who had married the Prince of Wales (later King Edward VII) in 1863. The Act provided for the incorporation of the company, with a capital of £600,000 and borrowing powers for a further £200,000, and powers to make the dock and six railways connecting it with the Monmouthshire Railway and the GWR. In addition, the B&MR was granted running powers over the authorised railways.

Great difficulties were experienced in attracting the necessary support for the projected dock. Matters were not helped by the unsettled financial climate which followed the Overend Gurney Bank crash of 10th May, 1866 and the ensuing panic in the markets. An important part was played by George Elliot (1815-1893), as described in his obituary in the *Proceedings of the Institution of Civil Engineers* in 1894:

> When the enterprise of local capitalists in the Alexandra Docks at Newport was flagging and the work of construction was at a standstill for want of funds, Sir George Elliot was induced to come forward, and from that time he evinced a great and practical interest in the undertaking.'

On 28th February, 1868, on the recommendation of its chairman, Lord Tredegar, George Elliot was elected to the board of the Alexandra (Newport) Dock (AD) Co.

George Elliot had been born in humble circumstances at Gateshead on 18th March, 1815. Starting work as a pit boy, he rose to the position of chief consulting and mining engineer to the Marquess of Londonderry. On 24th March, 1863 the pioneering South Wales colliery owner, Thomas Powell, died in Newport at the age of 83. Powell had developed pits at Gelligaer, Llantwit Fardre and, most important of all, in the Cynon Valley. Under the terms of his will his property passed to his three sons. Of these, Thomas Powell Jnr. chose to concentrate on the Llantwit Fardre house coal measures, while his brother Walter continued to work Gelligaer Colliery. However, all three were reluctant to take on the immense task of managing the most profitable part of the business, the steam coal pits of the Cynon Valley. George Elliot, together with fellow mining engineers T. E. Forster and William Armstrong, was called in to value the property. Elliot was so impressed with what he found that he arranged for the purchase of these collieries from the Powell brothers for £365,000.

On 28th July, 1864 the 'Powell Duffryn Steam Coal Co.' was registered to work the Duffryn, Aber-nant-y-groes, Aber-gwawr and Cwm Dare pits in the Cynon Valley, together with New Tredegar in the Rhymney Valley. George Elliot took over the supervision of the Powell Duffryn collieries as manager (1864-1877), later becoming managing director (1880-1886) and finally chairman (1886-1889). The Powell Duffryn Co. went on to acquire Ynyscynon and Treaman collieries in 1865, Fforchaman and Cwmreol from the United Merthyr Collieries Co. a year later, and in 1867 the Aberaman estate of Crawshay Bailey. However, even with this impressive portfolio, the company came close to dissolution in the depression of 1868-69. George Elliot was elected a member of the Institution of Civil Engineers in 1856 and created a Baronet in 1874 in recognition of his public services.

With George Elliot's vigorous support prospects for the new dock soon improved, and on 28th May, 1868 the ceremony of cutting its first sod was performed by Lady Tredegar 'amid general rejoicings', according to the report in the *Railway News* two days later. All places of business in Newport were closed for the day, with the inaugural event being followed by a breakfast 'numerously and influentially attended' and a grand display of fireworks. There was a note of caution, however, the promoters having announced that they intended to proceed with only one dock, leaving the other to wait until 'financial matters assume a more favourable aspect'.

The financial outlook for the dock company was further improved with the passing, on 25th June, 1868, of its second Act, which permitted the borrowing powers of the company to be exercised once one third (ie £200,000) of the capital authorised by the 1865 Act had been raised.

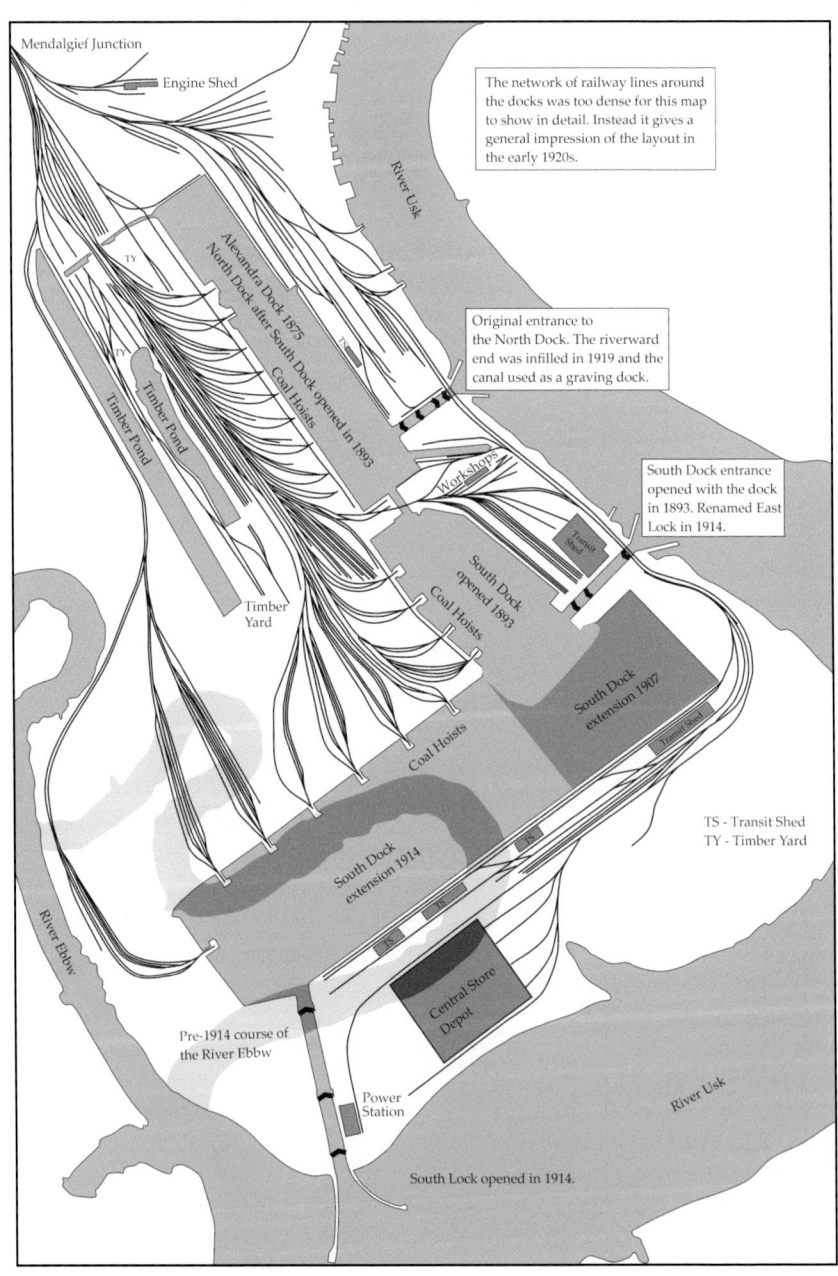

Progress on the construction of the new dock was very slow after 1868, however, with extensions of time for its completion being obtained under Acts of 9th August, 1870 and 21st July, 1873. In order to provide the necessary finance for the work, a limited liability company – the Newport (Alexandra) Dock Co. – was formed on 16th December, 1873 to lease the undertaking of the Alexandra Dock Co. The capital of the new company was set at £100,000, divided into 1,000 shares of £100 each, the principal shareholders listed in the Memorandum of Association of 13th December being Lord Tredegar (50 shares) and George Elliot (50 shares), with six other persons accounting for a further 50 shares. The lease, which was dated 17th December, was confirmed by the Alexandra (Newport) Dock Act of 16th July, 1874, which also sanctioned the raising of £150,000 of authorised capital by means of preference shares or stock, together with borrowing powers for a further £50,000. Under a later agreement, dated 16th December, 1879, the Alexandra Dock Co.'s undertaking was leased to the Newport (Alexandra) Dock Co. for a further period of 28 years from 1st January, 1880.

In addition, under Lord Tredegar's Supplemental Estate Act of 30th July, 1874 the trustees of his Lordship's estate were empowered to raise money on mortgage and to take shares in the Alexandra Dock Co. or the limited company to the value of £75,000. A similarly titled Act of 1878 enabled the trustees to take further shares in the dock company.

These arrangements provided the necessary financial basis on which construction could be pressed ahead, and the dock was opened to the accompaniment of great rejoicing by Mrs Benjamin Evans, Mayoress of Newport on 13th April, 1875. The new dock covered a deep water area of about 28¾ acres and measured 2,500 feet by 500 feet, with an average depth of 30 feet. During the remainder of 1875 982 vessels entered Alexandra Dock, with imports amounting to 107,180 tons, and exports (mainly coal) to 457,492 tons. By 1881 these totals had increased to 3,142 vessels, 595,757 tons of imports and 1,895,114 tons of exports, representing an increase in coal exports of about 400 per cent in six years.

Within days of this opening ceremony Charles Morgan III, the first Lord Tredegar, was dead, his title passing to his second son, Godfrey (1831-1913). Godfrey, who had been a captain in the 17th Lancers and had survived the Charge of the Light Brigade at Balaclava on 25th October, 1854, came to be regarded as a generous public benefactor who did much to develop education, health and recreational facilities in Newport. He became chairman of the Alexandra Dock Co., retaining this post until his death in 1913. Created the first Viscount Tredegar in 1905, Godfrey Morgan was made a Freeman of both Cardiff and Newport in 1909.

The new dock was served by two short lengths of railway, one from the Western Valleys line at Alexandra Dock Junction (Maesglas Junction from 1882) and the other from the South Wales main line at Western Valleys Junction (Alexandra Dock Junction from 1882).

Caerphilly Branch of the Brecon & Merthyr Railway

The Caerphilly branch of the Brecon & Merthyr Railway was authorised by the Rumney Railway Act of 1861. Construction had proceeded under the auspices of the B&MR, and on 1st February, 1864 its engineer reported that the works were 'nearly finished and this line will be opened for traffic very shortly'. However, this assessment proved somewhat over-optimistic as in their report to shareholders of 30th June, 1866 the Brecon & Merthyr directors were obliged to record that the branch was 'not yet open though almost complete'. According to this report, the opening had been postponed pending the completion of arrangements for the working of through standard gauge traffic between the Taff Vale Railway and Newport and because of a shortage of rolling stock. These statements must refer to the opening of this line through to its end-on junction with the Rhymney Railway at Van as the first coal to be dispatched by rail had left Rhos Llantwit Colliery, served by a siding off the branch about 3 miles to the west of Machen, for the B&MR main line in August 1864.

Another factor behind the delay in opening the Caerphilly branch throughout emerged in December 1868 when the Brecon & Merthyr Railway board agreed to the Rhymney Railway exercising its running powers to Rhos Llantwit Colliery 'so soon as the Rhymney put their line from Caerphilly to Walnut Tree Bridge into proper working order'. This must be a reference to the Rhymney Co.'s Caerphilly branch from Van to its junction with the main line at Penrhos.

The opening of the Cardiff and Caerphilly line in 1871 provided a more direct route for traffic off the Caerphilly branch of the B&MR, destined for Cardiff. Indeed, an important trade developed over these lines, as witnessed by *Herapath's Journal* of 29th July, 1871:

> A considerable traffic now passes over the narrow gauge route between Newport and Cardiff. This route is over the Monmouthshire to Bassaleg, the Brecon and Merthyr to Caerphilly Junction and the Rhymney thence to Cardiff. Although three companies have to be dealt with and the distance is 15 miles against 11 miles by the broad gauge, yet freighters appear to prefer it to incurring the expense of transhipment from the one gauge to the other.

However, this competitive advantage proved very short-lived, vanishing with the conversion of the South Wales main line to the standard gauge in May 1872. The Penrhos-Caerphilly West Junction line saw little traffic after the opening of the Cardiff and Caerphilly line and subsequently fell into disuse.

The B&MR also intended to run passenger trains over the Caerphilly branch: on 11th April, 1866 the directors resolved to take the steps necessary for the introduction of such a service. The following day notice of intention to open the line to passengers was forwarded to the Board of Trade, but little more appears to have been done until 15th February, 1867 when a committee of B&MR directors inspected the branch and the site of a proposed temporary station at Caerphilly. This facility would be necessary until the Rhymney Co. opened its new station on the Cardiff and Caerphilly line, then still under construction.

No more progress appears to have been made until 11th August, 1869 when the Brecon & Merthyr Railway directors agreed to proceed with the work of upgrading their Caerphilly branch for passenger traffic. This was taken in hand, and on 16th February, 1870 the company's engineer was able to announce that the line would be in proper order within a few days. Following his recommendation, a run round loop was ordered to be provided at the temporary platform at Caerphilly. The customary notices were forwarded to the Board of Trade and provision of the loop, together with an extension of the temporary platform, was reported to the Brecon & Merthyr Railway directors on 5th March.

The Caerphilly branch was inspected by Lt. Colonel Hutchinson for the Board of Trade, his report being dated 13th May, 1870. Unfortunately, Hutchinson was unable to support the sanctioning of the line for passenger use because of an unacceptable gradient of 1 in 60 through the temporary station at Caerphilly, together with the general incompleteness of the works. The Brecon & Merthyr Railway directors were outraged by this decision when it was reported to them, and reacted by ordering the sending of an indignant letter (dated 20th May) to the Board of Trade asking for Lt. Colonel Hutchinson's requirements to be reconsidered. On 7th June, after this missive failed to induce the hoped-for response, the company withdrew its notice of intention to open the branch to passengers.

The main problem was the temporary station at Caerphilly, which the Board of Trade was unlikely to sanction without major alterations. Further attempts to persuade the Board of Trade to the contrary proved equally unsuccessful, but rather more fruitful were the negotiations that followed for the use of the new Rhymney station at Caerphilly, which was opened on 1st April, 1871. The completion of the arrangement with the Rhymney Co. was reported to the B&MR board on 1st May, 1872.

This arrangement enabled a fresh notice of intention to open the Caerphilly branch to passengers to be forwarded to the Board of Trade on 24th September, 1872. In the event re-inspection by Colonel Hutchinson did not take place until the following Spring, his report being completed on 18th April, 1873. The Colonel found that the temporary station at Caerphilly had been abandoned and that B&MR trains would instead run into the new Rhymney station. The new works themselves were found to be satisfactory, apart from some minor and easily correctable defects, and so conditional approval was readily forthcoming.

All was now ready for a passenger service to be introduced between Caerphilly and Machen. On 29th May, 1873 the Brecon & Merthyr Railway traffic manager informed his directors that arrangements had been made to run special passenger trains over the branch on Whit Tuesday, 3rd June. However, an unexpected obstacle to the introduction of a regular service had also emerged. The Rhymney Co. was now demanding that B&MR passengers from the north of Deri, bound for Caerphilly and Cardiff, should be transferred to Rhymney trains at Bargoed, a requirement which would prevent the Brecon & Merthyr Railway making use of its Caerphilly branch as a route for such traffic.

The event that prompted the running of the special excursion trains over the Caerphilly branch on 3rd June, 1873 was a rehearsal at Caerphilly Castle by the South Wales Choral Union, fresh from their success at the Crystal Palace the previous year. The Brecon & Merthyr Railway trains were but a small part of a vast array of such trains attracted to Caerphilly, as described by the *Cardiff Times* of 7th June:

> The visitors began to arrive at Caerphilly before noon and from that time till late in the afternoon train after train disgorged crowds of excursionists from all parts of Glamorganshire and the three adjacent counties. Nearly thirty trains in all arrived during the morning and afternoon and comprised visitors from Merthyr, Aberdare, Abergavenny, Carmarthen, the Rhondda Valley, Rhymney, Brecon, Walnut Tree Bridge, Cardiff, Newport and the various intermediate stations between these towns and Caerphilly. Altogether no fewer than 12,000 to 15,000 persons were conveyed to Caerphilly and there is no doubt that number, large as it is, would have been doubled if the weather had been favourable.

The running of the inaugural trains over the Caerphilly branch was not, however, followed by the introduction of a regular passenger service, probably because of the Rhymney Co.'s continuing intransigence over the transfer traffic question. No further reference to this dispute has been found in the minute books of either company, so it would appear that the matter simply remained unresolved. So, despite its having been passed for passengers by the Board of Trade, the Caerphilly-Machen line stayed goods only, with occasional excursion traffic.

Pontypridd and Caerphilly: Early Schemes

The route provided by the Caerphilly branches of the Rhymney and Brecon & Merthyr Railways might, at first sight, have suggested the possibility of tapping the coal traffic of the Taff Vale Railway and diverting it to Newport by means of a northern curve at Walnut Tree Junction. However, this was hardly likely to be competitive given the heavy gradient, against the load, on the Rhymney line going north from this junction. To overcome this difficulty any connecting railway would have to start from much nearer Pontypridd in order to obtain a reasonably gentle climb up to join the Rhymney Railway near Penrhos. This was the approach adopted for most of the lines proposed over the years, although other ideas were also put forward.

The Brecon & Merthyr Railway was responsible for the earliest known proposal for a link between the Taff Vale Railway, north of Walnut Tree Junction, and the Rhymney Railway at Penrhos. In November 1863 the company deposited plans for various new railways, including lines from the Old Rumney, north of Bedwas, to Caerphilly, and from Penrhos to a junction with the Llantrissant & Taff Vale Junction Railway, the first section of which (from the Taff Vale Railway at Llantrisant Junction to Thomas Powell Jnr.'s Llantwit Colliery) had been opened on 17th September, 1863. The primary object of the Brecon & Merthyr Railway scheme appears to have been haematite iron ore traffic from the area to the south of Llantrisant, but a short spur (the 'Taff Vale Junction') was also proposed to connect with the main line of the TVR near Llantrisant Junction. The proposed lines were rejected by the legislature, but it is difficult to see how the Taff Vale Junction line could have provided an effective link between the TVR and the Rhymney Railway, given its adverse gradient up from the TVR main line.

The passing of the Alexandra (Newport) Dock Act in July 1865 created the incentive for a number of schemes for railways aimed at bridging the divide between the Rhymney Railway and the coalfield

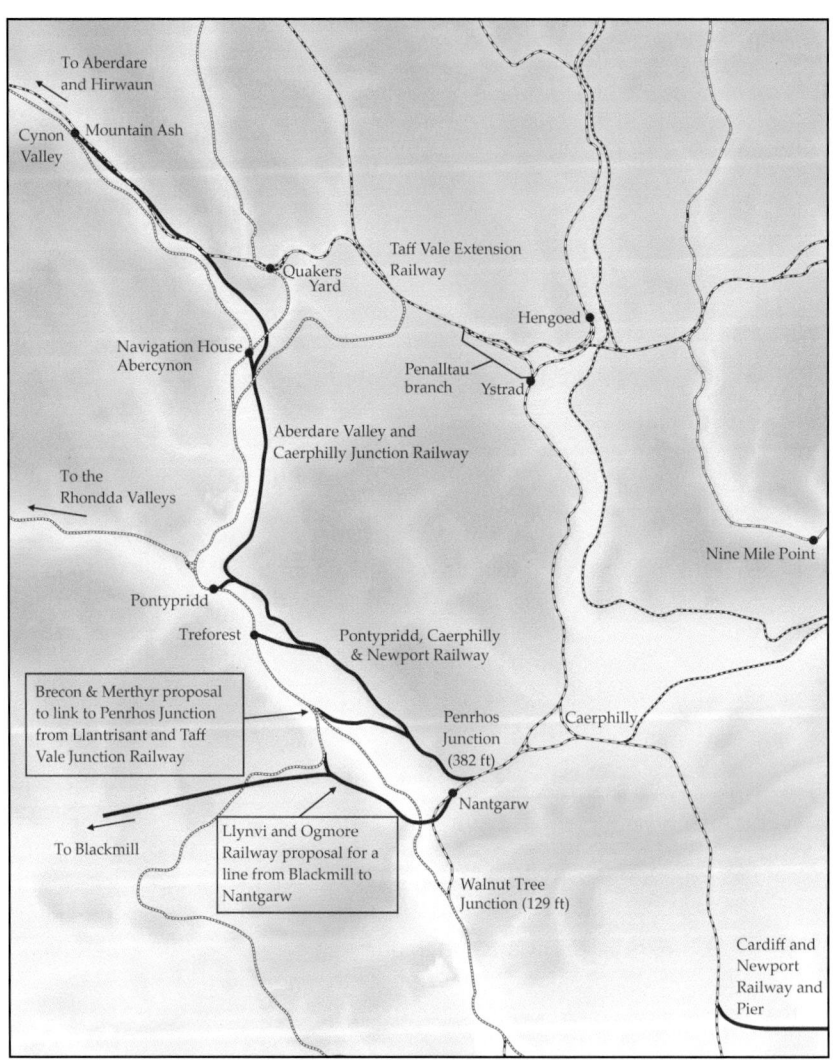

Pontypridd and Caerphilly: early schemes to connect the Rhondda and Cynon Valleys east to Caerphilly and Newport.
Relief shading contains OS data © Crown copyright and database right 2023.

valleys served by the TVR. On 18th July, 1865 the Rhymney board considered a proposal for the Aberdare Valley & Caerphilly Junction Railway (AV&CJR). Promoted by the Powell Duffryn Co., and in particular by its manager, George Elliot, together with colliery owner John Nixon, the Aberdare Valley & Caerphilly Junction Railway was to run from Mountain Ash, in the Cynon Valley, down the eastern side of the Taff Valley, to join the Rhymney Railway near Penrhos.

The Rhymney Co. was prepared to grant running powers over its line (except to Cardiff) in exchange for similar powers over the proposed railway. On 2nd November, 1865 George Elliot attended the Rhymney board meeting, but failed to persuade the directors to reduce the rates proposed to be charged on coal passing over their line from the proposed AV&CJR. Notice for the Aberdare Valley & Caerphilly Junction Railway Bill was published and plans deposited that month for the 1866 Parliamentary Session while negotiations continued between its promoters and their Rhymney counterparts. However, on 7th February, 1866 the Rhymney directors concluded that the AV&CJR proposals were 'inadmissible'. Faced with this impasse, the promoters withdrew their Bill, the Rhymney board being informed of this action on 1st June.

A rival scheme to the AV&CJR had been considered by the Rhymney directors at their meeting on 31st October, 1865. Put forward by Messrs Murray CE and Marsh and Cardiff solicitor R. W. Williams, and supported by Rowland Fothergill (then owner of the Taff Vale Ironworks at Pontypridd and the Abernant Ironworks at Aberdare, and a director of the Alexandra Dock Co.), Messrs Brown and Lenox (owners of a long-established chain works at Pontypridd) and Richard Bassett (a GWR director of Bonvilston, near Cowbridge, and promoter of a number of local schemes). This line was to run from a junction with the Taff Vale Railway, at Navigation House (Abercynon), to join the Rhymney Railway at Penrhos. The Rhymney Co. was asked to agree to work the proposed railway but on 2nd November its board refused to assist in its promotion, although it was intimated that traffic arrangements might be entered into in the event of an Act being obtained.

A third scheme for the 1866 Session came from a more established source. In November 1865 the Brecon & Merthyr Railway deposited plans for an ambitious programme of new works, entitled the 'Southern Lines'. Railway No. 9 of the Southern Lines Bill was to run from the Taff Vale Railway at Treforest to the Rhymney Railway at Penrhos, but this Bill was subsequently withdrawn.

A somewhat different approach was envisaged by another abortive scheme put forward at this time. The railway part of the Cardiff &

Newport Railway & Pier proposal would have run from a junction with the East Dock branch of the Rhymney Railway along the coastal plain, south of, and parallel to, the South Wales main line of the Great Western Railway, to the site of the authorised Alexandra Dock.

At this time some of the coal traffic from the Cynon Valley was being worked to Cardiff via the Taff Vale Extension line and the Rhymney Railway, by means of a reversal at Hengoed. A direct connection between these two railways would create a very attractive route for such traffic and be competitive with that provided by the TVR. On 1st June, 1866, following the withdrawal of the Aberdare Valley & Caerphilly Junction Railway scheme, the Powell Duffryn Co. suggested that the Rhymney Co. should seek running powers over the Vale of Neath and Taff Vale Extension lines from Aberdare and beyond. This the Rhymney board agreed to do, such powers between Hirwaun Pond and Hengoed being obtained in the Rhymney Railway Act of 12th August, 1867. However, these were not to be exercised until the Cardiff and Caerphilly line had been opened for traffic and the Great Western Railway had doubled its line to the west of Quakers Yard Tunnel (completed in 1868). The Act also authorised construction of a direct link, known as the Penalltau branch, between the Taff Vale Extension line, east of Llancaiach, and the Rhymney line at Ystrad (later Ystrad Mynach).

The Penalltau branch was opened as a single line only on 28th September, 1871, a second line being brought into use on 20th December, 1886. Whilst its main significance was as part of a competitive route for coal traffic from the Cynon Valley to Cardiff, via Caerphilly, the Penalltau branch also opened up the possibility of a new route to Newport taking in the Caerphilly branch of the B&MR.

The early 1870s witnessed further unsuccessful attempts to achieve a connection between the TVR north of Walnut Tree Junction and the Rhymney Railway at Penrhos. In November 1870, in a final attempt to break out of broad gauge encirclement, the standard gauge Llynvi & Ogmore Railway deposited plans for a grandiose venture comprising railways from its Ogmore Valley branch at Blackmill to join the Rhymney Railway near Nantgarw. This scheme would have included an 18-arch viaduct across the Taff's Well Gorge. It also featured a short spur, near Tonteg, which would have enabled traffic to pass from the Taff Vale Railway to the Rhymney Railway, via the Llantrissant & Taff Vale Junction Railway from Llantrisant Junction and the proposed railway. This latter route would have been somewhat indirect for trains from the Taff Vale Railway bound for Caerphilly and Newport and would also have suffered from the 1 in 40 climb on the Llantrissant &

Taff Vale Junction Railway up from Llantrisant Junction. However, the Great Western Railway, fearful of London & North Western Railway involvement in this project, agreed to convert its South Wales lines to the standard gauge, as a result of which the Llynvi & Ogmore Railway withdrew its Blackmill and Rhymney Bill.

Up to about 1870 ideas for a connecting railway between the Taff Vale Railway and the Rhymney Railway had focused principally on the prospect of attracting coal traffic from the Cynon Valley. A portent of the change of emphasis that was to occur later in the decade came on 10th October, 1871 when Messrs Davis and Pryce, solicitors of Cardiff, together with Mr Waller (a Cardiff contractor), placed a proposal for a railway connecting the Rhondda Valleys with the Rhymney line, near Nantgarw, before the Rhymney board. Although the Rhymney directors welcomed this scheme, they were not prepared to provide any pecuniary assistance towards its implementation.

An alternative route for coal traffic between the Cynon Valley and Newport became available in the 1870s. Between May 1873 and September 1874, under arrangements with the Sirhowy Railway and the Monmouthshire Railway & Canal Company, Great Western Railway coal trains from Aberdare bound for London and Basingstoke were worked via Hengoed and Nine Mile Point, with a backshunt at Waterloo Junction, Newport. This traffic was transferred to the Pontypool, Caerleon & Newport Railway on its opening on 17th September, 1874. However, this route was rather less direct and on 1st February, 1877, following agreement between the GWR and the LNWR, Aberdare to Newport coal trains reverted to that via Nine Mile Point.

The movement of coal from the Powell Duffryn Co.'s collieries in the Amman Valley, off the main Cynon Valley, to the Great Western Railway route to Newport was greatly facilitated by the opening of two short lines, from Treaman Siding to Middle Duffryn and to a junction with the Aberdare–Quakers Yard line of the GWR. Authorised under the Powell Duffryn Act of 18th July, 1872, the Powell Duffryn Railway enabled the colliery company's traffic to reach the GWR without needing to pass over Taff Vale Railway metals.

An unusual view of Machen station from the former B&MR line to Bedwas.
R. W. A. Jones

Chapter Three

Promotion and Construction

The years after 1865 saw a great upsurge in the output of the Rhondda coalfield in response to the rapidly growing demand for its 'Best Welsh' steam coal. High prices for this product following the Franco-Prussian War of 1870/71 and the so-called 'coal famine' of 1873 encouraged the sinking of new collieries and the expansion of existing ones. As a result by 1875 coal production in the Rhondda Valleys – then standing at 2,000,000 tons per annum – had exceeded that of the nearby Cynon Valley, the birthplace of the steam coal trade; by 1884 it was more than double.

The Rhondda Valleys, unlike that of the Cynon, had remained dependent upon the Taff Vale Railway and the Bute and Penarth Docks for the carriage of coal and its shipment. The tremendous growth in coal output, coupled with the failure of railway and dock accommodation to keep pace, led to severe congestion on the Taff Vale Railway main line and at the docks at Cardiff and Penarth. As a result, pressure mounted for improved facilities, particularly at the docks. However, this campaign received a severe rebuff when on 2nd November, 1876 the Marquess of Bute wrote to Cardiff Chamber of Commerce refusing to construct the Roath Dock, which had been authorised by the Bute Docks Act of 1874. This was followed, in late 1876 and the early part of 1877, by an attempt to promote a dock at Barry, together with connecting railways, but this abortive scheme failed to win the necessary support from the Great Western Railway and, most importantly, also lacked the backing of the colliery proprietors of the Rhondda Valleys.

Newport was seen by some as a possible alternative to Cardiff in the face of the intransigence of the Marquess of Bute and the growing needs of the export coal trade, especially as the opening of Alexandra Dock in 1875 had produced a very large surplus of capacity in relation to the traffic being handled there. It was argued that all that was needed to take advantage of this excellent facility was an efficient rail link between the Rhondda Valleys and Newport. Such a scheme was being discussed even before the failure of the Barry proposal in January 1877. An editorial in the *South Wales Daily News* of 23rd November, 1876, entitled 'Projected docks at Barry', noted that:

> Already there is talk of making a short line to join the Rhondda at its eastern extremity with the Brecon and Merthyr line, so as to bring Rhondda coal to Newport for shipment.

The key figures in the promotion of such a connection were Sir George Elliot and David Davies (1818-1890). According to Ivor Thomas, the biographer of David Davies, it was Davies who suggested to Sir George Elliot that a railway should be built from Pontypridd to Caerphilly. This line, in conjunction with running powers over the TVR, the Rhymney Railway and the B&MR, would put the Rhondda Valleys in direct communication with the docks at Newport. Davies, in his evidence before the House of Commons Committee on the Barry Dock and Railways Bill in 1883, stated that he had gone over the line with Sir George Elliot and had then 'marked out the route'. However, as we have seen, Sir George would have been very familiar with the idea of a railway along the lines suggested, having been a prime mover behind the Aberdare Valley & Caerphilly Junction Railway proposal of 1866.

David Davies, like Sir George Elliot, had come from very humble origins. Thanks to his business acumen and an uncanny knack for estimating quantities, he had moved from sawing timber into contracting, at first at a modest local level, and later into large-scale railway construction. Welsh railways built by Davies included the Oswestry & Newtown Railway, the Newtown & Machynlleth Railway, the Pembroke & Tenby Railway and the Manchester & Milford Railway. In 1864 he embarked on colliery development in the Rhondda Fawr Valley and by 1866 had, with partners, acquired some 8,000 acres of mineral property at Cwm-parc and Maendy. Given this interest, David Davies was anxious to secure an outlet for his steam coal free of the congestion encountered on the TVR and at Cardiff and Penarth Docks. He had played only a minor part in the abortive Barry scheme of 1875/76, but was to have a pivotal role in the promotion of the hugely successful Barry Dock & Railways, authorised in 1884.

The two men agreed to work together to promote the construction of a railway between Pontypridd and Newport, David Davies undertaking to subscribe £5,000 towards it, provided other Rhondda colliery owners found £15,000 between them. However, in a letter, dated 28th December, 1877, Davies was later to assert that he had also agreed with Sir George Elliot not to proceed with the scheme if the total subscription did not reach £45,000. Sir George was supported by his son-in-law, J. C. Parkinson, managing director of the Alexandra Dock Co. and a director of the Powell Duffryn Co. Parkinson was also president of Newport Chamber of Commerce and a forceful advocate of that port's advantages.

To facilitate the promotion of the new railway, J. R. Cobb of Brecon was appointed solicitor (he already undertook this role on behalf of the

B&MR), with James Weeks Szlumper (1834-1926) as engineer, the latter on the personal recommendation of David Davies.

A meeting between the promoters and their advisers was held on 19th July, 1877 to plan the campaign. The following day, J. R. Cobb wrote to Cornelius Lundie, manager of the Rhymney Railway, informing him that he had been instructed by 'gentlemen having control of an enormous amount of traffic from the Rhondda and Aberdare Valleys' to form a company to construct a railway between Pontypridd and the Caerphilly branch of the Brecon & Merthyr Railway. Between Penrhos and the intended junction with the Brecon & Merthyr Railway, the proposed line would run parallel to the Rhymney Railway, including the section from Penrhos to Caerphilly West Junction, which Cobb described as 'disused'. Alternatively, this 'disused' portion could be incorporated in the proposed railway. Cobb envisaged that the new line would prove beneficial to the Rhymney Co., but for it to flourish it must be free of any 'onerous charges'. He asked, therefore, if the company would be prepared to allow its Penrhos-Caerphilly West Junction line to be acquired by promoters of the new company.

Lundie's initial response, written on 21st July, 1877, was positive: he thought that his directors would view the proposed railway favourably, and that it would be best, for all parties, if use could be made of the Rhymney line. However, Lundie's board did not wish to part with any of its property for the benefit of the Pontypridd and Newport promoters, and on 1st August he informed Sir George Elliot of this decision, at the same time noting that his directors were not indisposed to granting running powers over the line in question. Meetings followed between the two men, but on 3rd November the Rhymney's board was informed that negotiations for running powers had reached an impasse.

The other company directly affected by the promotion of the new railway proved somewhat more receptive to its proposals. A letter from Sir George Elliot (dated 27th July, 1877), setting out the requirements for the proposed railway as they impinged upon the Brecon & Merthyr Railway, was considered by that company's board on 9th August. The Brecon & Merthyr Railway was willing to exchange running powers with, and to supply locomotive power for, the proposed railway, with the new company being responsible for carrying out improvements to avoid the adverse gradient at Machen, upon terms to be agreed for tolls and other charges. Negotiations proceeded on this basis but matters were not settled before the Bill reached Parliament.

On 14th November, 1877 the Alexandra Dock directors were appraised of the Pontypridd Caerphilly & Newport Railway proposal and its importance to the future prosperity of the company's dock, and agreed to give the scheme their full support.

The next step was to seek parliamentary authority, and on 16th November, 1877 a notice of the Pontypridd, Caerphilly & Newport Railway Bill was published, with powers being sought for four railways:

> Railway No. 1: from a junction with the TVR, south of Pontypridd to the Rhymney Railway, near the junction with that company's Caerphilly branch at Penrhos;
>
> Railway No. 2: from Railway No. 1 at Penrhos to a junction with the Caerphilly branch of the B&MR;
>
> Railway No. 3: from Railway No. 1, near Glyntaff, to Pont Shon Norton, north of Pontypridd; and
>
> Railway No. 4: a new line avoiding the climb up to Machen on the Caerphilly branch of the B&MR.

Railway No. 4 was to be vested, upon its completion, in the Brecon & Merthyr Railway Co. It was also intended to seek powers to enter into working and traffic agreements with the B&MR, TVR, GWR, LNWR and Rhymney Railway companies. Running powers were to be sought over the Rhymney Railway between Penrhos and the end-on junction with the Caerphilly branch of the B&MR at Van, the B&MR between Van and Bassaleg, and the TVR from the junction of Railway No. 1 to and over the Rhondda branches of that company. The new line was to be single track over most of its length and would make use of part of a disused siding which had linked the Taff Vale Ironworks at Treforest with the TVR at Pontypridd, in order to gain access to that railway. The plans for the PC&NR, deposited later that month, did not include Railway No. 3.

Also published in November 1877 was a notice for a Bill promoted by the Alexandra Dock Co. for a railway (No. 1) from the Tredegar Park Mile Railway to its docks lines, and (No. 2) from the B&MR at Bassaleg to a junction with the Tredegar Park Mile Railway, with running powers being sought over the Tredegar Park Mile Railway and the short section of the Western Valleys Line between Bassaleg and the commencement of the Tredegar Park Mile Railway. This proposal would have complemented the PC&NR, but was abandoned in January 1878.

There was already a rail link between Pontypridd and Newport, provided by the Taff Vale Railway main line, their Penarth Extension Railway and the Great Western Railway South Wales main line – over the Penarth North Curve (opened on 26th May, 1876). Although longer, this route offered gradients with the load from Pontypridd to Cardiff, and was virtually level from there to Newport, thereby enabling the working of heavier trains than would be the case with the PC&NR. Also, on 8th August, 1877, the GWR had entered into an agreement with the TVR (and the Rhymney Railway) aimed at the general elimination of hostilities between the companies. A response to the threat posed by the PC&NR scheme should not, therefore, have been difficult to foresee. When it came, it took the form of a joint reduction of the rates on coal and coke traffic from the TVR to Newport, via Penarth North Curve, significantly undercutting those envisaged for the PC&NR.

This was an extremely damaging blow to the prospects for the successful promotion of the Pontypridd, Caerphilly & Newport Railway; indeed but for the commitment of Sir George Elliot the project could well have collapsed at this point. It certainly proved too much for David Davies. On 7th January, 1878, he wrote to Sir George as follows:

> The Rhondda colliery proprietors having declined to take any interest in the Pontypridd and Newport line, I must do the same as I have no desire to enter upon an expensive contest without the aid of the Rhondda coal proprietors, nor do I believe the line will be made now the other railway companies have reduced the rate a ton as the new rate over the new line would be.

David Davies had gone into the question of rates to be charged via the PC&NR in some detail, but had found it impossible to make them competitive with those offered by the GWR and the TVR over the Penarth North Curve route. He asserted that he had only supported the PC&NR in his capacity as a colliery owner, and that the rate reduction had removed the incentive to construct the new railway. As a result, David Davies withdrew from the scheme, leaving Sir George Elliot alone to pursue the promotion of the PC&NR.

The PC&NR Bill had been introduced into Parliament on 21st December, 1877. It was opposed by the Great Western, Taff Vale, Brecon & Merthyr and Rhymney Railway companies, but supported by the Alexandra Dock Co. On 13th March, 1878 the directors of the last mentioned company resolved to give the Bill their full support in its passage through the House, including such expenses as might be necessary for the purpose. In addition, J. C. Parkinson, the dock company's managing director, was instructed to take the steps necessary to secure parliamentary authority for the Alexandra Dock Co. to subscribe £30,000 towards the capital of the PC&NR.

Public meetings were held to drum up support for the project. One held at the New Inn Hotel, Pontypridd on 20th March, 1878 was attended by J. C. Parkinson and James Szlumper, together with Francis

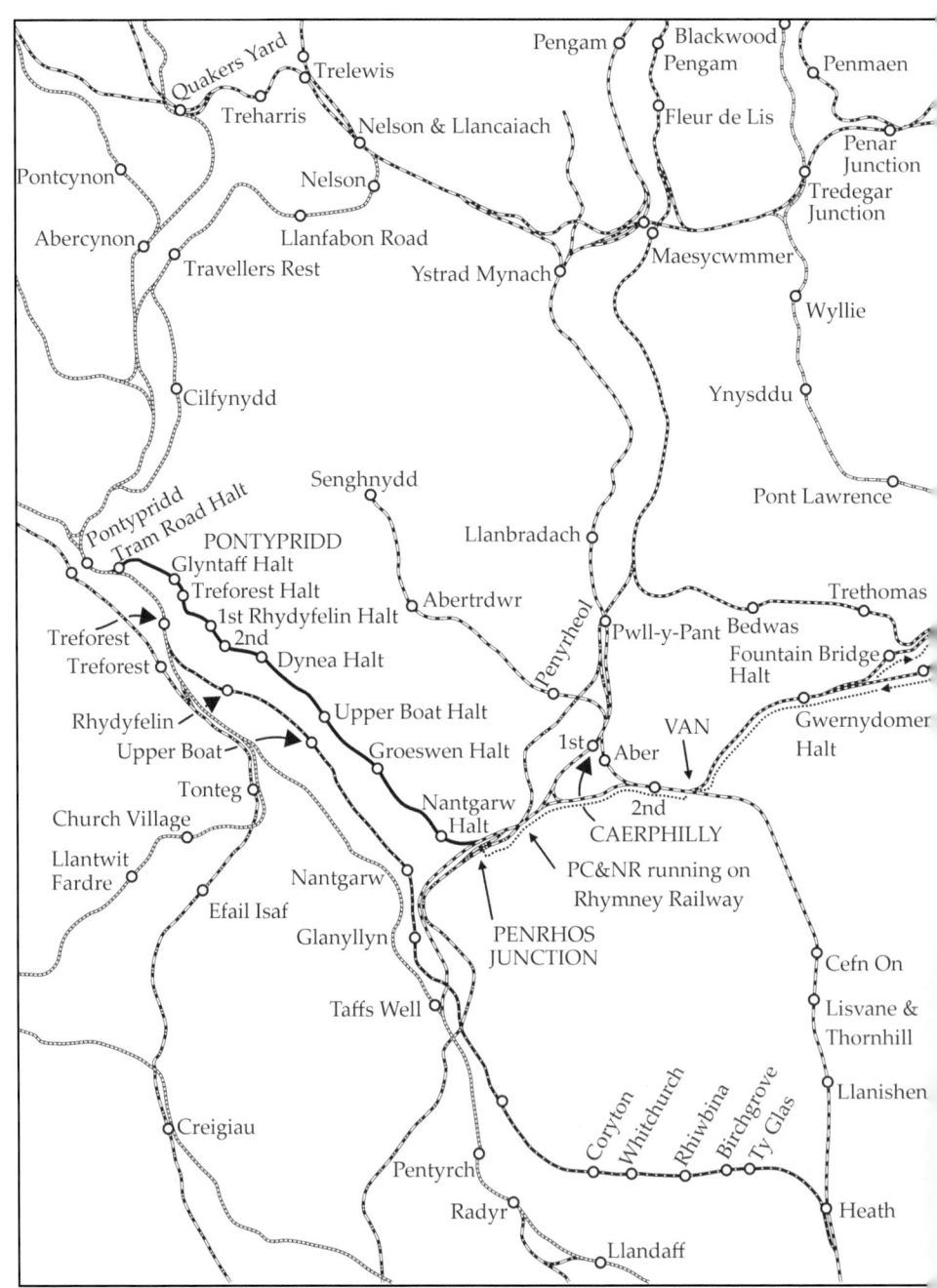

PROMOTION AND CONSTRUCTION

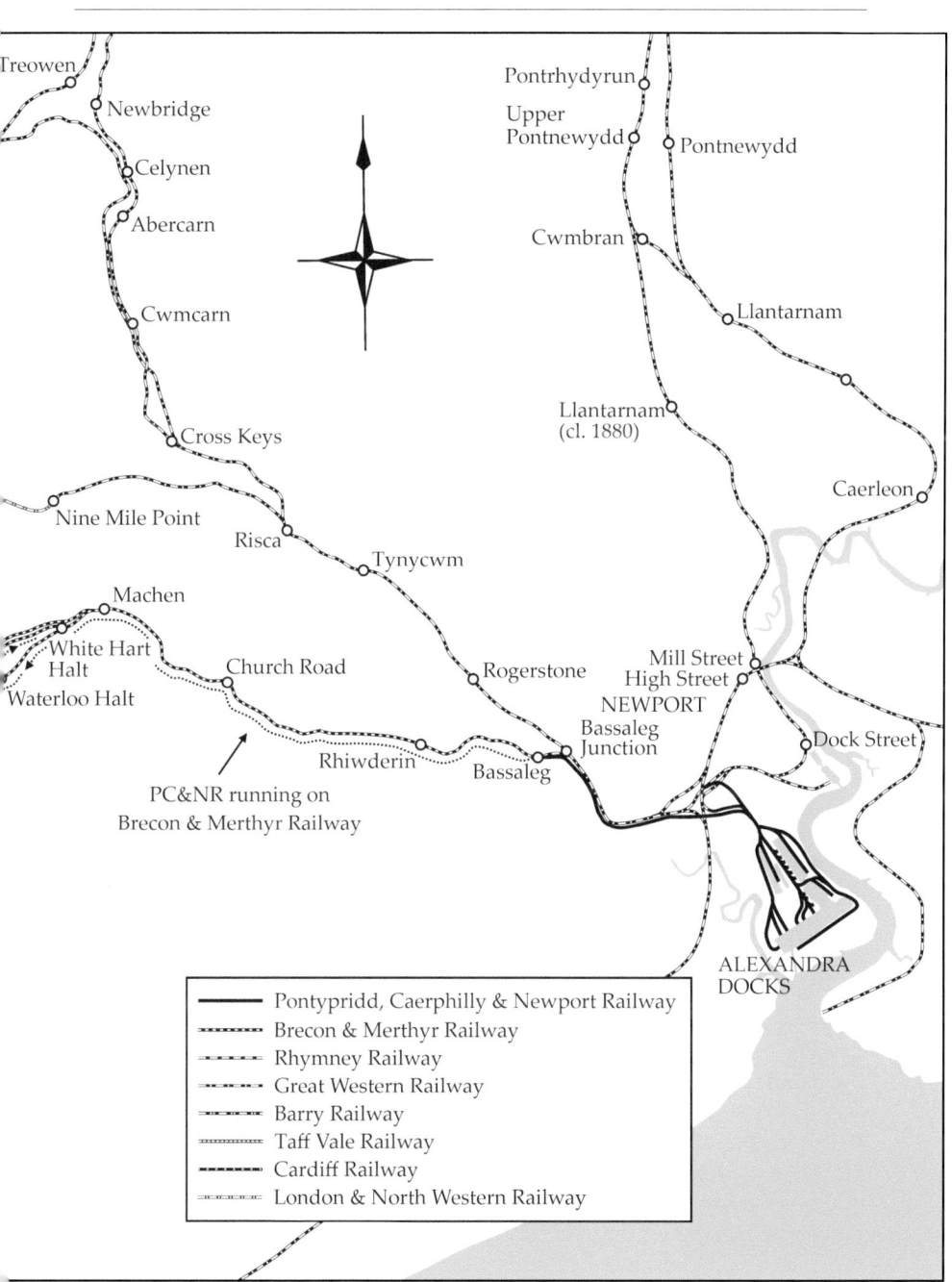

Crawshay of Treforest Iron Works, colliery owner Richard Cory and Gordon Lenox of the Pontypridd chainmakers Brown, Lenox & Co. This meeting and another held at Newport Town Hall on 1st April enthusiastically passed resolutions in support of the PC&NR Bill.

Efforts were also made to reduce the amount of opposition to the Bill. On 10th May, 1878 Sir George Elliot met George Fisher, general manager of the Taff Vale Railway, to put forward proposals. These were considered by the TVR board on 13th May, George Fisher being instructed to accept them if more favourable terms could be obtained. Further negotiations proved rewarding, with an agreement being entered into on 15th May. The TVR undertook to withdraw its petition against the Bill in return for the PC&NR abandoning its claim to running powers to and over the Rhondda branches. However, the TVR agreed to grant such powers into its Pontypridd station, and to provide reasonable facilities for the interchange of traffic and to convey such traffic to the new railway at rates per ton per mile no greater than those imposed on traffic passing over the TVR to Cardiff Dock.

An agreement (dated 16th May, 1878) was also reached with the Brecon & Merthyr Railway Co., whereby that company withdrew its objection to the PC&NR Bill. In addition to giving its support to the project, the B&MR was to grant running powers over its line between Caerphilly and Bassaleg in exchange for the same over the PC&NR. Similar powers were to be granted between Bassaleg and Newport 'so far as the Brecon Co. can grant the same', a telling phrase which was to return to haunt the two companies. Railway No. 4 was to be struck out of the Bill, but the B&MR Co. was to cooperate in the improvement or deviation of its line near Machen.

Unfortunately, agreement could not be reached with the Rhymney Co. for running powers between Penrhos and the Caerphilly branch of the Brecon & Merthyr Railway. The application for statutory powers for this purpose also proved unsuccessful.

The agreements with the TVR and B&MR Cos. ensured a much smoother passage for the PC&NR Bill than had been anticipated, the inquiry before the House of Commons Committee being adjourned so that the signing and other formalities could be completed. Having resumed its hearing the committee agreed the preamble to the Bill and various minor amendments on 16th May, 1878. Consideration by the House of Lords Committee took place in the following July, when strong opposition from the Marquess of Bute made its presence felt. Nevertheless, the Bill survived this onslaught largely unscathed, the most significant change being the deletion of a proposed clause which

PROMOTION AND CONSTRUCTION

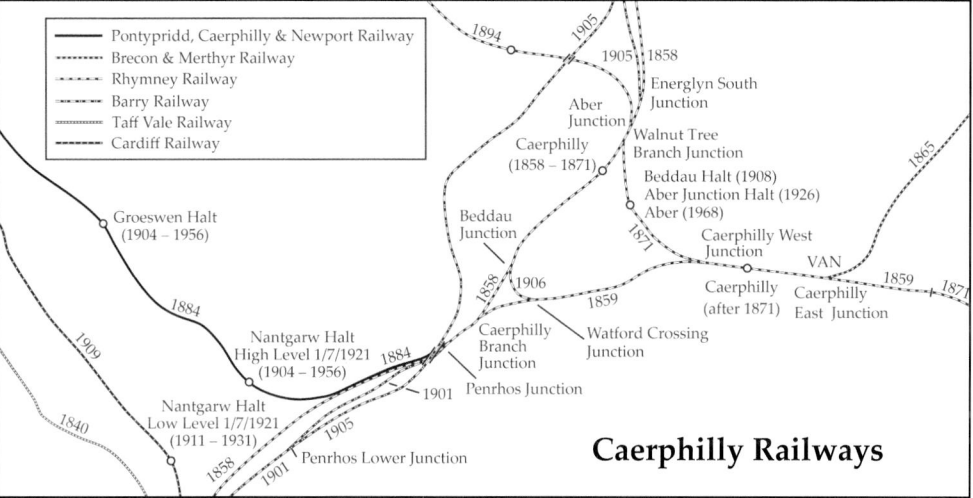

would have conferred powers on the Alexandra Dock Co. to subscribe towards the capital of the PC&NR Co. and to work the proposed line.

In celebration of the Bill's success a grand banquet for its promoters was held in Newport on 6th August, 1878 following the opening of a new graving dock earlier that day. The PC&NR Act received the Royal Assent on 8th August and provided for the incorporation of the company, with an authorised capital of £105,000, and borrowing powers for a further £35,000. Two railways were sanctioned: No. 1 from Pontypridd to Penrhos, and No. 2 from Penrhos to a junction with the Caerphilly branch of the B&MR. Three years were allowed for the compulsory purchase of property and five years for the completion of the works. The new company was granted running powers over the B&MR from the junction with Railway No. 2 to Bassaleg, and over the Rhymney line from Penrhos to Cardiff, via Caerphilly, but not through to the B&MR, the Rhymney Co. being granted similar powers over the authorised railways. The Act also confirmed the agreements with the TVR and the B&MR, both of which were scheduled to it.

The first directors of the company were named as Sir George Elliot, Crawshay Bailey Jnr. (senior having died in 1872) and James Ware. J. R. Cobb continued to act as solicitor, while on 7th August, 1878, J. C. Parkinson was appointed secretary and general manager of the PC&NR Co. However, the post of secretary was soon transferred to Edmund Creed.

On 7th December, 1878 a notice appeared in the *Railway Times*, inviting the submission of tenders for the construction of the PC&NR,

suggesting that work on the new railway would soon commence. However, this action proved somewhat premature, to say the least! In reality, the new company was experiencing great difficulty in attracting the financial support which was essential before construction could begin. In the event, only £8,500 was subscribed by the public out of the authorised capital of £105,000, the competitive rates introduced by the Taff Vale Railway and Great Western Railway proving a major disincentive to investors.

Fortunately, things improved markedly towards the end of 1880. On 23rd November Godfrey Morgan, the second Lord Tredegar, who had provided active support for the Pontypridd, Caerphilly & Newport Railway since the passage of its Bill through Parliament in 1878, was elected to the board of the new company. Also at the same meeting the directors were informed that arrangements had been agreed for the Newport (Alexandra) Dock Co., the limited company formed in 1873 to finance the construction of the dock, to subscribe the whole of the outstanding capital needed for the construction of Railway No. 1, as authorised by the PC&NR Act of 1878.

The following day a circular was published announcing that in view of the meagre response to the share issue, the PC&NR promoters had decided not to make any public allocation of shares and to return the limited number of applications that had been received.

The financial resources then available amounted to £80,400 out of an authorised capital of £105,000, only enough to complete Railway No. 1. This shortfall provided an opportunity for a legal challenge by the owner of a small quarry on the route of Railway No. 1 who wished to restrain the PC&NR from putting into effect its compulsory purchase powers as far as his land was concerned. In March 1881 the High Court judge found that the railway company's Act did not contain any authority for apportioning the capital between the two railways authorised, and therefore granted an injunction against the PC&NR.

To overcome this somewhat inconvenient obstacle it was arranged for an additional £24,600 to be subscribed towards the undertaking, this sum being made up of £12,300 from Lord Tredegar, with the balance divided evenly between Sir George Elliot's son George W. Elliot, MP for Northallerton, and J. C. Parkinson.

The strategic potential of the new railway had already been demonstrated before the ink was barely dry on its Act of incorporation. Intent on taking full advantage of the running powers contained in the PC&NR Act, the Rhymney Co. deposited plans in November 1878 for a total of seven railways running from a junction with the authorised railway at Glyntaff to serve Nixon's Navigation collieries at Mountain Ash and Merthyr Vale and the Castle Colliery of the Cyfarthfa Iron Co., near Troedyrhiw. The proposed line in the Taff Valley was to make use of part of the by then moribund Merthyr Tramroad and was also to connect with the private railway of the Cyfarthfa Co. The subsequent Bill was opposed by the Taff Vale Railway, which was also promoting its own scheme for a branch from its main line, north of Pontypridd, up the east side of the Taff Valley to Cilfynydd Inn and Stormstown, along much the same route as that proposed for the Rhymney extension. The Rhymney Bill was withdrawn after its first reading, following a vote against it at the company's half-yearly meeting of shareholders on 18th February, 1879. This left only the TVR branch (but only as far as Cilfynydd Inn) to be authorised by the Act of 21st July of that year. This line – known as the 'Pont Shon Norton branch' – was destined to serve the Albion Colliery at its terminus, from where the first marketable coal was raised in August 1887.

The TVR Bill had also been opposed by the PC&NR, which had succeeded in getting the following clause inserted in the resulting Act:

> If by agreement or otherwise the (TVR) Company carry or permit to be carried over their railway traffic destined for or coming from Newport or the docks at Newport at rates which shall be less per mile than the rates for the time being charged by the Company for like traffic to or from any dock or tidal harbour at Cardiff or Penarth, the Company shall carry like traffic to or from the railway of the PC&NR Co. (not destined for or coming from such dock or tidal harbour at Cardiff or Penarth) at rates per mile not exceeding such first-mentioned rates, and the PC&NR Co. shall in all respects be placed on at least as favourable a footing as any other company.

In 1877 the Taff Vale and Great Western railways had agreed to the introduction of a new through rate for coal and coke traffic from the former to Newport, via Penarth North Curve, aimed at undercutting those proposed by the PC&NR. The effect of the above clause was to render this alternative route quite useless. The PC&NR could now carry coal from the TVR to Newport at the same gross rate as applied in the case of traffic to Cardiff. The TVR and GWR would then have had to match this rate. However, as the route via Penarth North Curve was about 7 miles longer than that via the PC&NR, the rate per mile charged by the TVR and GWR would have been proportionately lower. The Taff Vale Railway would then have been obliged (under the terms of its agreement with the PC&NR of 15th May, 1878) to convey coal to the PC&NR at Pontypridd at this lower rate, something that company could not afford to contemplate. The competitive through rates via Penarth

North Curve remained in force during the construction of the PC&NR, but were withdrawn on the opening of the new railway in 1884.

Another possible avenue for an extension from the PC&NR was westwards, from Pontypridd into the Rhondda Valley. On 4th June, 1879 the *Western Mail* reported that a scheme was afoot to convert Dr Griffith's Tramroad (opened between Trehafod and the canal at Treforest in 1809) into a railway from a junction with the PC&NR at Treforest, but nothing came of this idea.

After its uncertain financial start, the Pontypridd, Caerphilly & Newport Railway faced another significant problem which needed to be addressed before work could begin on the new railway. At the Pontypridd end of the line use was to be made of a length of disused private railway between the Taff Vale Ironworks at Treforest and the Taff Vale Railway, where the connection with the main line east of Pontypridd station had been removed by 1877. Difficulties arose with the owners of the works, the Aberdare & Plymouth Co., which resulted in a deviation line being proposed to avoid this property altogether, bringing the junction with the TVR nearer to Pontypridd station. This change was authorised by the PC&NR Act of 12th August, 1880, three years being allowed for the completion of the deviation railway.

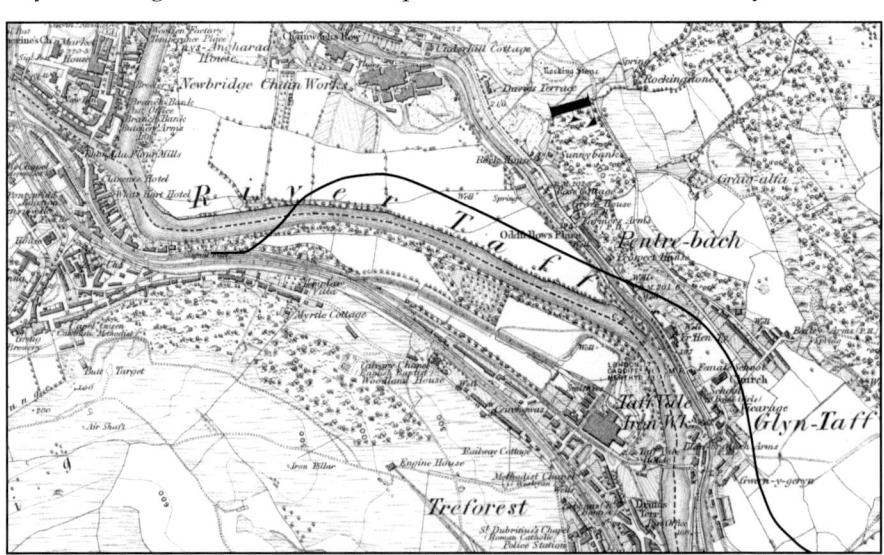

The original plan to link the PC&NR with the Taff Vale Railway involved using the siding that led to the Taff Vale Iron Works. The deviation line that was eventually built (the black line) created a new junction closer to Pontypridd.
© National Library of Scotland, adapted from the 1874 6 inch OS map, 2023.

This Act also included provision for a junction to serve the ironworks. In November 1890 the then owner of the works, James Lewis, obtained a court order confirming his right to have this junction made. This decision was affirmed by the Court of Appeal in May 1891, while on 18th November, 1892 the House of Lords dismissed an appeal against this ruling by the Pontypridd, Caerphilly & Newport Railway Co. However, it was not until just over three years later, on 5th February, 1895, that the PC&NR board gave instructions for such a connection to be made. Work at the site of the junction started on 11th February, when an engine and wagons arrived with earth to form an embankment. However, the siding itself was not constructed, although the abortive works cost over £480.

With the Taff Vale and Great Western railways' stranglehold on coal rates to Newport removed, its finances secure and the deviation line Act obtained, the PC&NR could finally begin to take shape. It was customary for the start of work on new railways to be commemorated by the cutting of the first sod, but the PC&NR was unusual in that two such ceremonies are recorded. The first took place on 21st December, 1880 in a field between Glyntaff Church and the Glamorganshire Canal, and was undertaken by Mr Allen and Mr Snipe, officers of the railway company, before a crowd of enthusiastic spectators.

The second ceremony occurred on 8th April, 1881 in a field near Glyntaff Cemetery and appears to have been held at the instigation of the contractor, John Mackay. Also present were Messrs Armstrong and Gardiner, engineers respectively of the GWR and the LNWR, and other unnamed friends of Mr Mackay. The Rev. Jones, Vicar of Glyntaff, blessed the occasion with some appropriate words, and then the party adjourned to a nearby inn for the customary refreshments. Work is reported to have started in earnest later that afternoon.

However, it was not until 6th May, 1881 that the PC&NR board was informed that tenders having been invited for the construction of Railway No. 1 (from Pontypridd to Penrhos), that of John Mackay of Hereford (at £64,300) appeared to be the most beneficial. Mackay had been responsible for the Morlais Tunnel on the LNWR near Dowlais and a junction railway at Landore. Notices to treat had been served on all landowners, with negotiations as to the price of the land under way in most cases.

In June 1881 it was reported that the hard rock cutting at Glyntaff was being blasted out by Mr Mackay, and that this was providing suitable stone for the viaduct over the River Taff, near Pontypridd. This viaduct was the most significant structure on the line, comprising three spans of wrought-iron girders resting on stone piers and abutments. To the south of Glyntaff progress was much easier given the level and loamy nature of the ground. In order to provide a constant ruling gradient of 1 in 200 up to the junction with the Rhymney Railway at Penrhos, the route of the new railway climbed gradually up the hillside on the east side of the Taff Valley with substantial cuttings being required on the approach to and at this junction. Although originally intended as a single line, the PC&NR was constructed as a double track railway throughout.

Powers for the compulsory purchase of land required for the construction of Railway No. 2 (the PC&NR's authorised line between Penrhos and the Caerphilly branch of the B&MR) were due to lapse on 8th August, 1881, but negotiations had continued with the Rhymney Co. for the use of its line between those points. These bore fruit in the form of an agreement, dated 5th August, which, in addition to granting the necessary running powers, also provided for the abandonment of Railway No. 2 and the refurbishment of the Rhymney line between Penrhos and Caerphilly West Junction. The Rhymney Co. was to lay a second line of rails over this section when, in the opinion of an independent arbitrator, the traffic of the PC&NR was unduly hindered by single line working. This agreement was confirmed by the PC&NR Act of 10th August, 1882, the Act also authorising the abandonment of Railway No. 2.

Also enacted in the same Session was the Alexandra (Newport & South Wales) Docks & Railway Act, which received Royal Assent on 18th August, 1882. In addition to authorising the dock company's change of name, this Act also contained powers for building a second dock, to be known as the 'South Dock', together with an additional £300,000 capital and borrowing powers for a further £100,000. The Act also empowered the PC&NR Co. to subscribe £50,000 towards the dock undertaking.

The Alexandra (Newport & South Wales) Docks & Railway Bill had also unsuccessfully sought running powers over the GWR and the Tredegar Park Mile Railway, between Bassaleg and Maesglas Junctions. These were eventually obtained, together with similar powers over the Western Valleys Line and the B&MR between Rhymney and Bassaleg Junction and between Van and Machen, under the AD&R Act of 31st July, 1885. Reciprocal running powers in respect of the lines of the AD&R and the PC&NR were granted under the AD&R Act of 25th July, 1890.

In spite of these developments, dissatisfaction with the facilities available for the transport and shipment of Rhondda coal continued to mount. As a result a group of colliery proprietors, led by David Davies, John Cory and Archibald Hood, combined to promote the construction of a new dock at Barry, together with a direct rail link to the Rhondda Valleys. A rival scheme was also brought forward for a dock at the mouth of the River Ogmore, south of Bridgend, which could be connected to the

Rhondda Valleys if the Great Western Railway could be persuaded to build the railways between Porth and Hendreforgan, near Tonyrefail, authorised by its Act of 1882.

Bills for the Barry Dock & Railways and the Ogmore Dock and Railway were deposited in November for the 1883 Session of Parliament. The threat these schemes posed for the PC&NR will be readily apparent, and in the same Session that company sought to consolidate its somewhat vulnerable position by promoting extensions to its system. In its Parliamentary Notice, published on 15th November, 1882, it proposed to seek powers for a total of six new railways, made up of two principal elements:

- From the PC&NR at Glyntaff into the Cynon Valley, making use of Nixon's Private Railway, to a junction with the Powell Duffryn Railway at Aberaman, with running powers over the former;
- From the B&MR at Bassaleg to Alexandra Dock and the GWR at Newport, independently of the TPMR, but with running powers also being sought over that railway and the adjoining lines of the GWR.

The 1883 Session saw one of the great parliamentary battles of Welsh railway history. The Barry Dock & Railways scheme was eventually rejected by the House of Lords Committee, while the Ogmore Dock & Railway was authorised by Act of 20th August. The PC&NR's fortunes, on the other hand, proved somewhat mixed. Its Bill had been opposed by the GWR, the TVR and by Lord Tredegar. The extension into the Cynon Valley failed because the House of Commons Committee was unwilling to grant powers over Nixon's Private Railway on the grounds that the land on which it was constructed was only leased by the colliery company. The independent line from Bassaleg to Alexandra Dock, which had been opposed by Lord Tredegar, was sanctioned subject to a number of clauses designed to protect his Lordship's interests. The latter's opposition had been withdrawn on the PC&NR promoters agreeing to these clauses and to pay the same tolls over the projected railway through Tredegar Park as were paid by the GWR over the existing line.

The resulting Act, which received the Royal Assent on 2nd August, 1883, also gave the PC&NR Co. the right to enter into working and traffic agreements with the Alexandra Docks & Railway, Brecon & Merthyr Railway and Lord Tredegar, and authorised a further increase of capital of £45,000, together with borrowing powers for an extra £15,000.

Prior to the passing of this Act an agreement had been entered into between the Pontypridd, Caerphilly & Newport Railway, John Nixon and the Powell Duffryn Co., whereby Nixon was to build his private railway from his Navigation Colliery at Mountain Ash to a point near the Aberdare Canal basin, where an end-on junction was to be effected with the railway company's proposed Cynon Valley extension. The failure of this part of the PC&NR Bill left Nixon without a southern outlet for his railway. He was forced, therefore, to look to the TVR to provide this connection, a junction between the two lines being brought into use in November 1884 under an agreement dated 31st March of that year.

Also opened in November 1884 was a new connection between the Aberdare branch of the Taff Vale Railway, near Abercwmboi Siding, and the Powell Duffryn Co.'s Middle Duffryn Sidings. This provided a direct link to the Taff Vale Railway from Middle Duffryn Colliery and, via the Powell Duffryn Railway, the collieries of the Amman Valley.

The 1884 Parliamentary Session witnessed a re-run of the Barry Dock & Railways battle of the previous year. Once again the Barry scheme was faced with competitive proposals. The Ogmore Dock & Railway promoters returned with a scheme for a direct railway from their authorised line to Pontypridd – the Pontypridd & Ogmore Railway – but this was abandoned before the Bill could be printed. Also proposed in this Session was the Rhondda & Bristol Channel Railway, the moving forces behind which were Sir George Elliot and W. T. Lewis (1837-1914), later first Baron Merthyr of Senghenydd, and manager of the Bute Estate since 1880. The Notice of the Bill, dated 13th November, 1883, gave details of eight railways, which can be grouped into three main parts:

- From Cwmpark in the Rhondda Fawr Valley to a junction with the PC&NR at Glyntaff;
- From a junction with the PC&NR just below Glyntaff to the South Wales main line, near Pengam, with a short spur to the Cardiff and Caerphilly line of the Rhymney Railway;
- From the South Wales main line at a point between Marshfield and Alexandra Dock Junction to Alexandra Dock.

Running powers were to be sought over the Taff Vale, Rhymney and Great Western railways, together with the short section of the Pontypridd, Caerphilly & Newport Railway at Glyntaff.

The Rhondda & Bristol Channel Railway was a strange amalgam of otherwise competing interests. While the proposal suggests a certain lack of confidence in the prospects for the PC&NR on the part of that railway's chief promoter, Sir George Elliot, it would also have countered the Barry scheme. Indeed, in June 1884 Sir George candidly admitted that it had been promoted for the purpose of 'bringing to their senses other railway companies'. For the Bute side the link to the Rhymney Railway would have established a route to Cardiff competitive with that of the TVR, similar to that later envisaged for the Cardiff Railway. The proposed railway was welcomed by the Alexandra Docks & Railway board on 14th December, 1883, when the company's managing director, '...explained fully...the advantages to the Alexandra Docks and the District of this additional independent line of railway between the Rhondda and Aberdare Valleys and the Ports of Cardiff and Newport'.

In spite of this endorsement, the Rhondda & Bristol Channel Railway was not to be, as the Bill itself fell foul of the Standing Orders of the House in March 1884. The second attempt to promote the Barry Dock & Railways, on the other hand, proved rather more successful, the scheme being authorised by Act of 14th August, 1884 and the new dock opening on 18th July, 1889.

The promotion of both schemes posed a major threat to the future wellbeing of the TVR, which was likely to lose a considerable portion of its revenue as a result of traffic diverting from its main line to a new railway. The clear message for the company was that it should avoid fighting on two fronts. Accordingly, an accommodation was reached with the PC&NR, under which the TVR undertook, in an agreement dated 20th June, 1884, to provide locomotive power and work the goods and mineral traffic of the PC&NR, in trains of not less that 25 wagons, between Pontypridd and Bassaleg, pending the opening of the independent line to Alexandra Dock. This agreement was to remain in force for 10 years from 1st July, 1884, after which it was to be subject to 6 months notice by either party.

Sir George Elliot was able to announce the signing of this agreement during his appearance later that same day before the House of Commons Committee considering the Barry Dock & Railways Bill. He denied that it was an attempt 'to throw dust in the eyes' of the committee, but confirmed that the agreement would, by making use of the PC&NR's running powers over the Rhymney Railway, provide an alternative route between Pontypridd and Cardiff, via Caerphilly (although through traffic does not appear to have ever been worked via this route).

Meanwhile, work had been continuing on the Pontypridd, Caerphilly & Newport Railway. This had proceeded in two main portions: southwards from Treforest and northwards from the Rhymney Railway at Penrhos. In February 1883 it was reported that in spite of unfavourable weather over the previous five or six months, good progress had been made, and that the two sections had met at Ffynon Wen, near Nantgarw. In addition, the Rhymney Co. had proceeded with the rehabilitation of its Penrhos-Caerphilly West Junction line, that company's shareholders being informed at their half-yearly meeting on 17th August, 1883, that while this had not resulted in any aditional capital expenditure, it had produced a small increase in working expenses.

On 11th January, 1883, the Taff Vale Railway board had considered a letter from Sir George Elliot applying for the junction at Pontypridd to be put in. However, the directors were not prepared to accede to this request until a proper agreement had been entered into, although they raised no objection to Sir George putting in the junction at his own expense, if he so wished. The necessary agreement was soon arranged and approved by the Taff Vale Railway board on 19th February. The new junction was inspected by Colonel Rich, who, in his report to the Board of Trade of 30th April, was unable to recommend approval because of the incompleteness of the works. However, by the time of his re-inspection on 8th June the deficiencies had been remedied, with the junction points ready to be connected once approval had been granted, which it was. Unfortunately, prospects for the early opening of the railway received a setback early in 1884 when it was reported that because of a defect it had been found necessary to dismantle and rebuild one of the abutments of the Taff Viaduct at Pontypridd.

Traffic to and from the PC&NR, when it opened, would have to pass over the Brecon & Merthyr Railway main line, east of Machen, which was only single line. In their half-yearly report to shareholders in August 1882 the Brecon & Merthyr Railway directors had forewarned that:

> Having regard to the very large increase in traffic which it is anticipated will take place over this Company's system upon the completion of the PC&NR, the Directors have instructed the Engineer of the Company to at once prepare the necessary plans and estimates for the doubling of the line from Bassaleg Junction northwards'.

Plans and estimates for the doubling of the line between Machen and Bassaleg were submitted to the Brecon & Merthyr Railway board on 26th September, 1882, when the company's engineer was instructed to commence the work in the cuttings at Machen and near Bassaleg.

On 28th March, 1884 the Brecon & Merthyr Railway notified the Board of Trade that this widening would be ready for inspection on 1st April. Colonel Rich inspected the new works and recommended, in his report of 3rd April, that conditional sanction be granted, subject to re-inspection of the signalling and locking arrangements and the slopes of a cutting to the west of Bassaleg station. Subsequent re-inspections did not satisfy the Colonel on this latter point, and it was not until 11th January, 1886 that he felt able to recommend final approval for the new works. Nevertheless, on 23rd April, 1884 the Brecon & Merthyr Railway secretary had been instructed to advise Sir George Elliot of the completion of the doubling and of his company's readiness to carry the PC&NR Co.'s traffic.

Chapter Four

Open to Traffic

Opening to Goods

By the middle of 1884 the three principal requirements for the successful opening of the PC&NR were all in place: Railway No. 1 between Pontypridd and Penrhos Junction was complete; the Brecon & Merthyr Railway main line had been widened between Machen and Bassaleg; and the Taff Vale Railway had agreed to provide engines and work the traffic. However, the incline west of Machen and the Bassaleg-Alexandra Dock line still remained to be dealt with, while the question of running powers over the GWR beyond Bassaleg Junction had not been satisfactorily resolved. Indeed, on 23rd June, 1884 the GWR refused to countenance any variation in the B&MR's running powers over this section, as contained in the existing agreement between the two companies.

Nevertheless, arrangements went ahead for the opening of the PC&NR. Board of Trade Inspection of the line was not required because passenger trains were not to be run. On 4th July, 1884, the *South Wales Daily News* reported that 50 of the more experienced Taff Vale Railway guards and brakesmen, together with a number of drivers and firemen were to be transferred to work the traffic of the new railway.

Monday, 7th July, 1884 was set as the date for the official opening. The inaugural train, consisting of 25 loaded coal wagons, was worked down from the Powell Duffryn Co.'s collieries in the Cynon Valley. Driven by David Thomas, reputedly the oldest driver on the TVR with 43 years service, the train passed onto the PC&NR at Pontypridd at 11.00 am. On board, representing the TVR, were James Hurman, traffic manager, H. O. Fisher, engineer, inspector Davies of Treherbert and other officials of the company, together with J. C. Parkinson of the PC&NR Co. The train paused at Caerphilly for a B&MR engine to be put on to assist between there and Machen, a symbolic and practical gesture, while the opening party were joined by Alfred Henshaw, traffic manager of the B&MR.

At Bassaleg Junction the train came to a halt. Alfred Henshaw tendered a 'permit' to work over the GWR beyond the junction, but an official of that company refused to recognise it or allow the train to pass. According to the *South Wales Daily News* 'the contretemps may be better imagined than described'. At length, the train was moved to a nearby siding, the TVR engine returning light to Pontypridd. Their plans thwarted, the opening party proceeded to Newport 'by other means', meeting at the King's Head Hotel to enjoy 'a sumptuous cold collation'.

These events were considered at the Great Western Railway board meeting on Wednesday, 16th July, 1884, when the directors were informed that their chairman, Sir Daniel Gooch, had met Sir George Elliot, J. C. Parkinson and Edmund Creed, the PC&NR secretary, to discuss the question, the inaugural train having been tendered 'without previous arrangements having been made'. Sir George had stated that the arrangements being sought were of a temporary nature pending the completion of his company's independent line to Alexandra Dock. In response, the GWR board undertook to convey the PC&NR traffic from Bassaleg Junction on such a basis (on terms to be agreed), subject to an understanding being reached as to the accommodation to be provided at the junction. Accordingly, the 25 wagons of coal, which had remained at Bassaleg since the 7th July, were moved to the dock by a GWR engine on the afternoon of the board meeting.

A further meeting between representatives of the two companies took place at Westminster on 19th July, 1884. Henry Lambert, the GWR's chief goods manager, wished to see two sidings provided for the PC&NR traffic on the B&MR at Bassaleg. Edmund Creed, on the other hand, felt that only if any difficulties arose should such accommodation be provided. The GWR officers suggested that the matter should go to arbitration, but this was rejected by the PC&NR side.

Regular traffic over the Pontypridd, Caerphilly & Newport Railway, bound for Bassaleg and exchange with the GWR, commenced on 25th

Alexandra Docks & Railway locomotive delivering timber at Treforest, c. 1910.

Author's collection

July, 1884. However, three days later the *South Wales Daily News* reported that two trains had been stopped at Bassaleg, with a third standing in a siding at Pontypridd. On 30th July the GWR board heard that the PC&NR had, without any arrangement having been concluded and in spite of the GWR's views concerning the inadequacy of facilities at Bassaleg, continued to leave trains on the B&MR main line for exchange with the GWR. This traffic had been worked forward by the GWR, albeit with considerable difficulty, but the PC&NR and the B&MR had been warned that unless proper interchange facilities were provided it would be impossible for this practice to continue.

The dispute was addressed again at a meeting between the GWR general manager, James Grierson, Alfred Henshaw, Sir George Elliot and others interested in the PC&NR on 12th August, 1884. Mr Henshaw felt that up to ten trains might be exchanged daily without undue delays, provided the B&MR put on staff at night, which he agreed to do. He also proposed that loaded wagons should be placed in an existing B&MR siding at Bassaleg, for collection by the GWR, with that company's engines leaving the empty wagons on the B&MR main line to the west of Bassaleg Junction. When the GWR objected to this last point, Henshaw suggested that the empties could be worked to a siding on the B&MR.

The general manager's report of this meeting was considered by the GWR board on 13th August, 1884, when it was agreed that the company's engines could work to and from the B&MR sidings with up to five trains each way daily. However, despite this the PC&NR traffic continued to be worked in the old way. On 24th September the B&MR directors, having heard that this traffic was increasing, with eight full loads having been sent down in one day, that the GWR was still being obstructive, and that the TVR had complained of delays, resolved to take the matter up with the GWR. Finally, on 4th December the GWR board was informed that the B&MR had conceded that things could be improved if the traffic was handled at its sidings to the west of Bassaleg Junction. This having been settled, the new mode of exchange was introduced, with a consequent reduction in delays to the PC&NR traffic.

Bassaleg-Alexandra Dock

Problems with the Great Western Railway could be avoided altogether once the PC&NR's independent route from Bassaleg to Alexandra Dock, authorised by the Act of 1883, became available. However, the provision of this short length of railway was to be beset by complex legal wrangles resulting from a somewhat bizarre confrontation between the PC&NR Co. and Lord Tredegar, the latter acting in defence of his rights and property at Tredegar Park, whilst at the same time being deputy chairman of the company promoting the new line.

The authorised railway was to extend from a junction with the B&MR at Bassaleg to join the dock lines of the AD&R, with its central portion through Tredegar Park running parallel to and to the south-west of the Tredegar Park Mile Railway. Work on the sections outside the park had commenced by 15th August, 1884, when progress was reported to the PC&NR shareholders at their half-yearly meeting in London. On 25th August the B&MR board agreed arrangements enabling the PC&NR's contractor to pass over that company's line and for making a temporary junction at Bassaleg. However, it was not until 22nd October that B&MR's general manager was given authority to determine the precise position of this junction. Unfortunately, these encouraging signs were not to be a pointer for the early completion of the new railway.

The Bassaleg-Alexandra Dock line had been opposed by Lord Tredegar, with the result that a number of protective clauses had been inserted in the PC&NR Act, which had received the Royal Assent on 2nd August, 1883. The powers for the authorised railway through Tredegar Park were to be suspended for one year from the passing of this Act, and were not to be exercised at all if Lord Tredegar completed the new lines or widened the Tredegar Park Mile Railway within 18 months of that

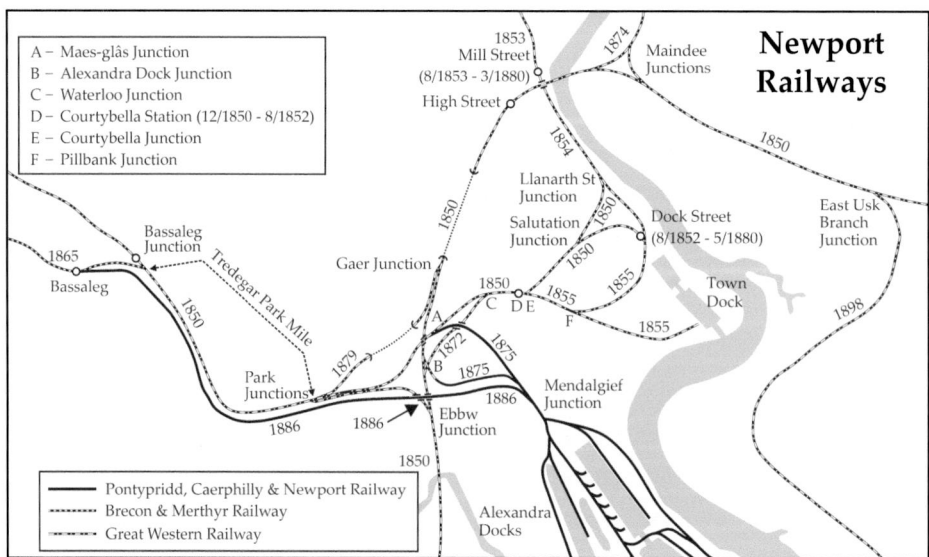

date. Alternatively, his Lordship could give up the existing TPMR to the PC&NR in lieu of the latter's authorised railway or the widening of the TPMR. The PC&NR would then be obliged to complete, at its own expense, a third double line of rails to the north-east of earthworks already formed by Lord Tredegar for the second line of rails alongside the Tredegar Park Mile Railway, when required to do so by the GWR.

However, if Lord Tredegar did not, within one year of the passing of the Act, take such steps as would ensure the provision of the additional lines for the PC&NR within the 18 months deadline already referred to, or had not given up the existing Tredegar Park Mile Railway to the PC&NR within this period, then the suspension of powers for the latter's independent line would cease. In any event, the PC&NR was to pay tolls to his Lordship on all traffic passing through Tredegar Park. These were to be fixed by agreement, but were not to exceed 1*d.* per ton per mile or the lowest such rate charged over the PC&NR.

To understand the implications of these provisions and the complex developments which followed the passing of the 1883 Act it will be helpful to outline the equally complex history of the TPMR.

The TPMR had originally been sanctioned as a tramroad by Act of 1802, the tolls paid over the years to the Morgans of Tredegar Park contributing in no small measure to that family's vast fortune and causing this section of line to be known as the 'Golden Mile'.

On 7th November, 1874 the GWR published a Notice for a Bill seeking powers for the construction of four railways from the confusingly initialled Pontypool, Caerleon & Newport Railway to Cross Keys and a junction with the Sirhowy Railway, avoiding the TPMR and its tolls altogether. The Bill was opposed by the Monmouthshire Railway & Canal Co. and also, not surprisingly, by the first Lord Tredegar. However, under an agreement with the MR&C Co., dated 15th June, 1875, the GWR undertook not to construct the four railways, if authorised by Parliament, in exchange for the MR&C Co. granting running powers over all of its lines as from 1st August of that year. Another agreement, entered into between the GWR and Lord Tredegar on 17th June, 1875, provided for the granting of similar powers over the TPMR, his Lordship being required, when called upon by the GWR, to construct two additional lines of rails alongside the TPMR.

The GWR Act of 19th July, 1875 authorised the construction of the four railways from the Pontypool Caerleon & Newport Railway, but the powers for these were to be suspended if, within three years, Lord Tredegar provided the two additional lines of rails referred to in his agreement with the GWR. In anticipation of such a requirement emanating from that company, Lord Tredegar had the earthworks formed for the additional lines to the north-east of his existing railway. This work involved the cutting away of rising ground alongside the Tredegar Park Mile Railway to the same level as that line. However, at this stage no rails were laid on the new earthworks.

On 13th July, 1883, during the passage of the PC&NR Bill, a second agreement was entered into between the GWR and Lord Tredegar, which permitted his Lordship to transfer that company's traffic onto the lines to be laid on the earthworks already referred to. In return, Lord Tredegar was to provide, within 12 months of being required to do so by the GWR, two further lines to the north-east of these earthworks. This arrangement would enable Lord Tredegar to dedicate the original TPMR for use by the PC&NR, thereby avoiding the need for that company to build its proposed independent line through Tredegar Park.

On 10th September, 1883 the GWR served notice on Lord Tredegar requiring him to complete the additional lines of rails referred to in their agreements of 1875 and 1883. His Lordship then proceeded to have the two lines of rails laid on the earthworks already formed to the north-east of the TPMR, leaving the connections at each end to be put in, when required, to bring about the diversion of GWR traffic onto the new route.

Lord Tredegar gave notice to the PC&NR on 11th June, 1884 that the two additional lines of rails had been laid, that he was ready to construct two further lines to the north-east of these, as required by the PC&NR Act 1883, and that on completion of this third set of double lines the PC&NR could have exclusive use of the original TPMR.

The PC&NR responded to this notice on 19th June, 1884 by asserting that it showed that Lord Tredegar had not in fact given up the existing Tredegar Park Mile Railway, nor did he intend doing so within the time limit specified in the company's Act of 1883. The railway company also argued that the laying of rails on the earthworks to the north-east of the TPMR was not a 'widening' within the meaning of that Act, but was work that had been carried out for and at the request of the GWR.

No doubt fearful of the consequences of Lord Tredegar's intervention, the PC&NR also embarked on what was to be an unsuccessful attempt to secure parliamentary powers aimed at circumventing any obstacle that his Lordship might seek to put in the way of the company's direct access to Alexandra Dock. The notice for this Bill, published in November 1884, sought running powers over the Western Valleys Line south of Bassaleg Junction, the TPMR and the dock lines of the AD&R, together with authority to enter into working and traffic agreements with Lord Tredegar and the AD&R, B&MR and GWR Cos.

A further notice was served by Lord Tredegar on the PC&NR on 21st January, 1885, stating that he had completed the two additional lines of rails through Tredegar Park and that he was prepared, on and after 31st January, to give up the existing TPMR for use by the PC&NR. This would be just within the 18 months deadline set by the 1883 Act.

However, the PC&NR was still anxious to have its own railway rather than be dependent on one provided by his Lordship. On 3rd February, 1885, the day after the deadline in question, a letter was sent from the PC&NR's solicitors to those of Lord Tredegar stating that the company had been advised 'on high authority' that it was still entitled to make its own railway through Tredegar Park, as authorised by the Act of 1883. This letter repeated the views set out in the PC&NR's response to Lord Tredegar's notice of 11th June, 1884 and enclosed notices to treat in respect of land belonging to Lord Tredegar which was to be acquired compulsorily for the construction of the independent railway. A further notice, dated 8th April, 1885, advised his Lordship that the railway company intended to take possession of the land in question.

Lord Tredegar's response to this threat was to institute legal proceedings, on 14th April, 1885, to restrain the PC&NR from taking possession of his land, claiming loss of tolls and likely 'disfigurement' of Tredegar Park itself. As a result, his Lordship was granted an interlocutory injunction against the PC&NR, and on 1st August he returned to court with the object of confirming this ruling. On 24th August the PC&NR directors were informed that the injunction had been granted and that the company's solicitors had been instructed to lodge an appeal.

While this action was proceeding a meeting took place between Lord Tredegar and Sir George Elliot, following an Alexandra Docks & Railway board meeting on 1st September, 1885, at which the latter offered to purchase the original Tredegar Park Mile Railway. The following day Sir George wrote to his Lordship setting out his understanding of this conversation: he had assumed that Lord Tredegar was agreeable to his suggestion and on this basis he had given instructions for the connections with the new PC&NR lines to be put in at each end of the TPMR.

This letter did not produce any immediate response from Lord Tredegar or his advisers, and so preparations went ahead for the provision of these connections. The GWR had already applied, on 29th August, 1885, for Board of Trade sanction for the new section of double line to the north-east of the original TPMR. The new works were inspected by Colonel Rich, his report being completed on 5th September. Colonel Rich found the new railway in place but not connected up to the

Great Western Railway lines at either end. He also noted that the new PC&NR lines, which were to form continuations from the extremities of the original Tredegar Park Mile Railway to Bassaleg and Alexandra Dock, were still under construction. Rich concluded that the arrangements, although not operational, were nevertheless satisfactory and so recommended the Board of Trade to sanction the making of the connections referred to and their bringing into use.

As recorded by Colonel Rich, work was also proceeding with the construction of the new PC&NR line from its junction with the B&MR at Bassaleg to the northern end of the Park Mile. Early completion of this link was highly desirable as it could be used to bring down materials for the extension of the railway from the southern limit of the TPMR through to Alexandra Dock. On 11th October, 1885 the B&MR completed the facing crossover near the site of the intended junction to the east of Bassaleg station, and on 25th October the permanent connection with the new PC&NR line was put in. The GWR then connected up its Western Valleys Line to the new lines to the north-east of the original TPMR, leaving the latter to be joined up to and used by the PC&NR

These actions triggered a rapid and indignant response from Lord Tredegar's solicitors. On 26th October, 1885 Messrs Carlisle and Odell wrote to the Pontypridd, Caerphilly & Newport Railway stating that there was no arrangement in place between the railway company and Lord Tredegar and pointing out that the original Tredegar Park Mile Railway could only be taken in accordance with the provisions of that company's Act of 1883. Faced with such forthright opposition Sir George Elliot gave instructions that no further use should be made of the new connections until such time as the dispute had been settled.

Lord Tredegar's solicitors wrote again on 30th October, 1885, stating that any use of the new connections, even for temporary purposes, had to be on a 'without prejudice' basis, but this was rejected by the Pontypridd, Caerphilly & Newport Railway side. Faced with a potentially damaging impasse on this point the railway company adopted a more conciliatory tone, and on 6th November a letter was sent to Lord Tredegar stressing the mutual advantages that would result from early completion of the independent route to the dock and arguing that use of the new connections for construction purposes could not possibly prejudice his Lordship's rights. The letter concluded by asserting that:

> ...the present case is one which ought to find a friendly settlement, and we are satisfied that the Directors of the Company earnestly desire to put an end to all litigation and differences with Lord Tredegar.

This olive branch provided the much-needed impetus for further negotiations and for an understanding concerning the temporary use of the connections in question. On 29th January, 1886 the PC&NR directors were informed that their line from the southern end of the Tredegar Park Mile Railway through to Alexandra Dock was being 'pushed on vigorously towards completion.'

Finally on 16th March, 1886 the PC&NR solicitors wrote to their opposite numbers setting out a basis for settlement of the dispute. They proposed that the railway company would now acknowledge that its right to make an independent railway alongside the Tredegar Park Mile Railway had ceased on the grounds that Lord Tredegar had, within one year of the passing of the 1883 Act, substantially commenced to widen and lay down additional rails on the Tredegar Park Mile for use by the PC&NR.

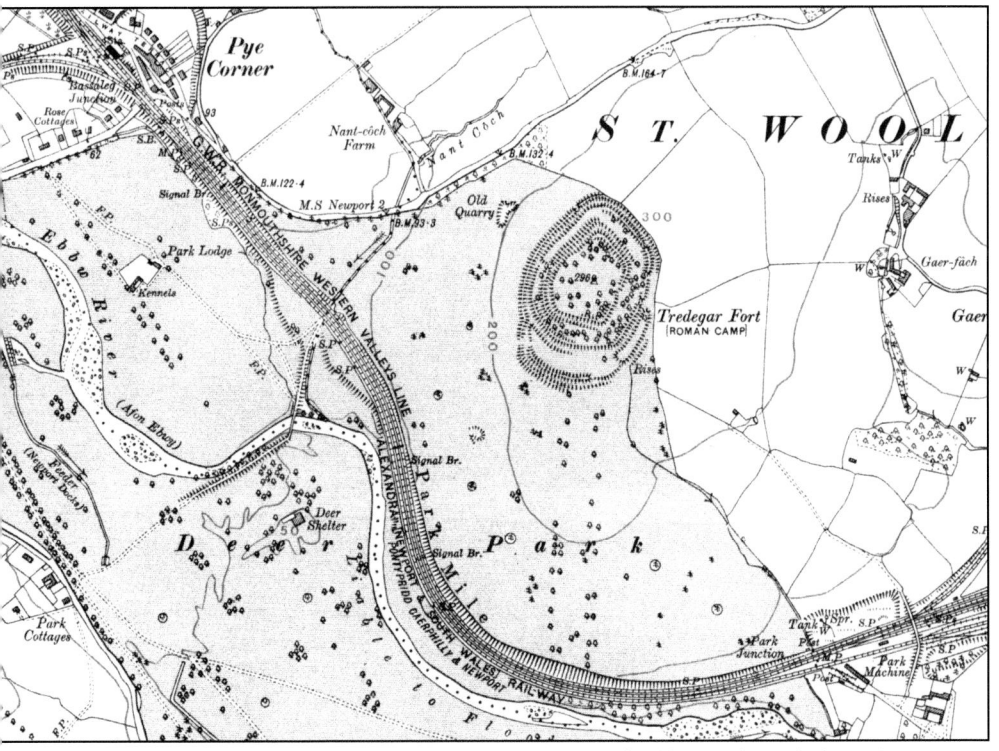

The route through Tredegar Park. The 1922 map shows the final layout through the Park Mile with the three double track lines sharing the same corridor. The 1886 PC&NR line to the south and west; the 1899 GWR one to the north and east on land prepared for its construction in 1875; and the original line running between them.

© National Library of Scotland, adapted from the 1922 6 inch OS map, 2023.

This concession was sufficient to break the logjam and arrangements went ahead for the opening of the Bassaleg-Alexandra Dock line for traffic. Although the junction for the PC&NR at Bassaleg had been put in in October 1885 it was not until 10th March, 1886 that the B&MR applied for Board of Trade sanction for its use, the works being expected to be ready for inspection on 15th March. Once again this task was carried out by Colonel Rich, his report of 16th March recommending that approval be given, subject to certain minor alterations. The following day Alfred Henshaw informed the B&MR traffic & works committee that the PC&NR had asked to be allowed to bring the new line into use. This being agreed, the Bassaleg-Alexandra Dock line was opened to goods and mineral traffic only on 18th March.

However, under arrangements introduced the following day the Taff Vale Railway continued to leave PC&NR traffic at Bassaleg, from where it was worked by AD&R engines to Alexandra Dock, via the independent line through Tredegar Park. This practice, which remained in force for the next 19 months, was necessary pending the completion of Mendalgief storage sidings at the southern end of the line. It was not until 28th September, 1887 that the TVR's traffic manager, James Hurman, was able to report that this route was available throughout and that the PC&NR had asked the TVR to work the Alexandra Dock traffic direct to the new storage sidings. This, Hurman felt, would be of great benefit to the TVR, avoiding the delays which resulted from the limited accommodation available at Bassaleg, as well as effecting other savings. However, for the sake of economy, it would be desirable to stable two TVR engines at the AD&R shed at Newport. To this end Hurman had been to Newport with Tom Hurry Riches, the TVR locomotive superintendent, and had found the locomotive accommodation there to be satisfactory. These recommendations having been accepted by the board, TVR engines commenced working the PC&NR coal trains right through to the Mendalgief storage sidings on 19th October, 1887.

Despite these practical developments the legal action by Lord Tredegar to restrain the PC&NR from taking possession of his lands in Tredegar Park for railway purposes had remained unresolved, although one complication had been set to one side. On 2nd June, 1886 the GWR board had agreed to negotiate a deferral of its requirement for the construction of the third set of rails through Tredegar Park, as set out in its notice to Lord Tredegar of 10th September, 1883.

However, on a somewhat less positive note, on 8th June, 1887 Lord Tredegar had commenced a fresh action against the PC&NR, this time for the recovery from the company of unpaid tolls for its use of the original TPMR. This case was heard in the High Court on 27th March, 1889, and on 3rd April judgement was given in favour of his Lordship, the PC&NR being found liable for payment of the outstanding tolls, the settlement of the accounts being referred to the Official Referee.

The PC&NR appealed against this judgement, but fortunately further negotiations led to the resolution of this protracted dispute by way of an agreement entered into between the company and Lord Tredegar on 24th April, 1891. Under the terms of this agreement the PC&NR abandoned its appeal and accepted the tolls judgement, with each side agreeing to pay half the costs of constructing the additional lines through Tredegar Park, when these were required by the GWR.

A postscript to these events occurred in December 1892 when the PC&NR published a notice for a Bill proposing the provision of two connections, one at each end of the TPMR, which would have enabled GWR trains to make use of the lines already used by the Pontypridd company, thereby avoiding the need for the construction of a third double line of rails through Tredegar Park. However, the GWR was having none of this and so the Bill was withdrawn early in 1893.

Opening to Passengers

Although the primary objective behind the promotion of the PC&NR had been the carriage of coal from the TVR at Pontypridd to Alexandra Dock, the line also provided a direct connection between three important centres of population. So it is not surprising that, with the goods and mineral business established, thoughts turned to the prospects for a passenger service over the new railway. On 6th February, 1886 the PC&NR directors made a special inspection of their line, which, it was announced, was to be opened to passengers as soon as certain alterations had been made. In addition to the PC&NR itself, a Pontypridd-Caerphilly-Newport passenger train service would need to run over two other goods-only sections – that of the Rhymney Railway between Penrhos Junction and Caerphilly West Junction and that of the B&MR between Caerphilly and Machen – both of which needed to be upgraded to passenger standards.

It was also necessary for the various lines to be submitted to the Board of Trade for approval before passenger trains could be run. The first to be inspected was the Rhymney line, which was reported on by Colonel F. H. Rich on 20th December, 1886. However, Colonel Rich concluded that sanction should be withheld because of the incompleteness of this single line section, in particular the need for a lodge for a gatekeeper at

Watford Crossing, midway between Penrhos Junction and Caerphilly West Junction. Final sanction was not granted until 9th December, 1887, following the submission of undertakings concerning the lodge in question and the mode of working the single line railway.

Colonel Rich also inspected the Pontypridd, Caerphilly & Newport Railway itself, his report of 19th February, 1887 stating:

> I have the honour to report for the information of the Board of Trade that in compliance with the instructions contained in your Minute of 10th ult., I have inspected the PC&NR from its junction with the TVR near Pontypridd to a junction with the Rhymney Railway at Penrhos, near Caerphilly.
>
> It is a double line, 5 miles 11 chains long, the gauge is 4 ft 8½ inches and the intervals between the lines of rails and between the railway and the sidings are not less than 6 feet.
>
> The permanent way consists of a Vignoles (ie flat-bottomed) pattern rail, which is fished and fixed with fang bolts and clips to sleepers laid transversely about 3 feet apart, except those near the rail joints which are about 2 ft 2 inches apart. The line is ballasted with slag and broken stone, and fenced with post and rail and post and wire.
>
> The ruling gradient is 1 in 200 and the sharpest curves, which are reported to be 10 chains radius, are provided with check rails.
>
> There are no stations or public level crossings on the railway, but there are siding junctions at Penygroes and at the quarry. The signals and points at these junctions are interlocked, and are worked from adjacent cabins.
>
> There are five brick arches over the line and two wooden ones that carry the occupation roads, five brick and stone underbridges and four that have stone abutments and wrought iron girders, plus two viaducts, the one over the River Taff at Pontypridd, and the second over the public road and canal. These have stone piers and abutments and wrought iron girders. The widest of these is 69 feet... ...I could not test the wrought iron girders for want of the necessary means to do so...

The report went on to identify a number of requirements, including the need to strengthen two wooden occupation bridges, to improve the communications between the signal cabins, to provide a repeater to the down distant signal at Penygroes and to lift and ballast the railway in the cutting near Penrhos Junction. As a result, Colonel Rich concluded that the line 'cannot be opened for passenger traffic without danger to the public using the same'. By the time of his re-inspection on 12th December, 1887, however, these deficiencies had been put right and he was therefore able to recommend that final sanction be granted for the running of passenger trains over the PC&NR.

The Caerphilly branch of the Brecon & Merthyr Railway had already (in May 1873) been passed for passenger use by the Board of Trade.

Carriages Nos. 1 and 3 of the of PC&NR, built for them and photographed by the Gloucester Railway Carriage and Wagon Company. *Author's collection*

However, a short tunnel near Gwuan-y-Bara on this line was still in need of some attention. On 14th October, 1887 the B&MR engineer was instructed to prepare plans and estimates for the tunnel's widening, together with other works for the accommodation of passenger trains over the branch line. The alterations at the tunnel (estimated to cost £630) were approved by the company's traffic & works committee on 19th October, and were ordered to be carried out at once.

It was also necessary to arrange terms and conditions for the use of the other railway companies' stations at Pontypridd, Caerphilly and Newport. An agreement with the Taff Vale Railway, dated 21st November, 1887 provided for the use of Pontypridd station and the carrying out of the alterations required by the Taff Vale Railway, principally the construction of a bay platform. That with the Great Western Railway, dated 1st December, 1887, was limited to the working of three Pontypridd, Caerphilly & Newport Railway passenger trains into and out of Newport (High Street) station each day (except Sundays).

With the various arrangements completed, the Pontypridd, Caerphilly & Newport Railway was ready to introduce its passenger train service. On 20th December, 1887 James Hurman informed the Taff Vale Railway board that he had agreed, subject to confirmation by his directors, for the Pontypridd, Caerphilly & Newport Railway passenger service to start on 28th December, with that company's train temporarily making use of the main line platforms at Pontypridd pending completion of the new bay line and platform.

Hurman's action having been endorsed by his directors, the Pontypridd, Caerphilly & Newport Railway passenger service duly commenced on the date proposed, the first train leaving Pontypridd, without ceremony, at 8.35 am, and arriving at Newport 50 minutes later. Formal inauguration was reserved for the second train of the day, the 9.50 am from Newport, which conveyed Sir George Elliot and 'a large number of influential gentlemen connected with the trade and mercantile interests of Newport and the district' (*South Wales Daily News*). The train and its prestigious load were met at Pontypridd by James Hurman and his assistant Mr Page, representing the Taff Vale Railway, these two gentlemen having come up from Cardiff for the purpose.

The Pontypridd, Caerphilly & Newport Railway board meeting on 10th January, 1888 was an occasion for self-congratulation following the successful opening of the line to passengers. The directors also confirmed the appointment of Alfred Henshaw as the company's traffic manager. This role was to be additional to Henshaw's duties in the same capacity with the Brecon & Merthyr Railway, a post he was to retain until 1894. One of his first tasks was to report on requests that had been received for stations at Upper Boat, Groesfaen and Nantgarw, between Pontypridd and Caerphilly, together with one at Gwaun-y-Bara on the Caerphilly branch of the B&MR. Having pointed out that the district served by the PC&NR was mainly agricultural and sparsely populated, Henshaw concluded that any stations were likely to prove unremunerative and could not be recommended. His views were accepted by the PC&NR board at its meeting on 27th February, 1888, and so the passenger trains continued to run between Pontypridd and Caerphilly without calling at any intermediate stations.

Under the PC&NR Act of 1878 the Rhymney Railway had been granted running powers between Pontypridd and Penrhos Junction. However, these were of little use without facilities for the interchange of traffic with the TVR. Therefore, in the 1886 Session the Rhymney Co. sought power 'to require the PC&NR to construct, maintain and work at the junction of their railway with the railway of the TVR Co. at Pontypridd proper and sufficient sidings in connection with that junction'. The Bill itself was carried over into the following Session, as a result of the dissolution of Parliament, and was not enacted until 29th

Carriage No. 4 of the PC&NR built by the Gloucester Railway Carriage and Wagon Company. *Author's collection*

March, 1887. The required sidings were to be completed within 18 months of the passing of the Act, but it was not until 10th January, 1888, following considerable pressure from the Rhymney Co., that the PC&NR board gave instructions for them to be laid. The connections to the 'Interchange Sidings' were reported to be ready for inspection on 10th December and were the subject of a favourable report made by Colonel Rich to the Board of Trade on 18th December.

Machen Loop Line

Even though the operating efficiency of the PC&NR had improved considerably with the introduction of through working between Pontypridd and the Mendalgief Dock storage sidings in October 1887, the route was still hampered by single line working between Penrhos Junction and Caerphilly West Junction, and between Caerphilly and Machen, the latter section including the adverse gradient west of Machen. The PC&NR Act of 1878 had included a short line (Railway No. 4) at Machen, aimed at improving the situation, but this had been struck out following the agreement between the PC&NR and B&MR of 16th May of that year. This provided that until the B&MR line was improved to give a gradient of 1 in 176, the PC&NR would pay for any additional haulage required at the incline. The B&MR was, when called upon by the PC&NR, to carry out improvements at Machen, with the cost to be apportioned between the two companies.

The Pontypridd, Caerphilly & Newport Railway's next move was to seek to acquire the Caerphilly branch from the Brecon & Merthyr Railway. This question was discussed by the B&MR directors on 25th August, 1881 when it was agreed to consider any proposal put forward by Sir George Elliot. However, Sir George's offer, when it appeared, did not come up to expectations, the B&MR traffic & works committee of 2nd November finding it 'quite inadequate', with the estimates of traffic and profits being much lower than had been anticipated.

Following this rebuff and clearly not content with the existing arrangement with the Brecon & Merthyr Railway, the PC&NR proceeded, later that month, to deposit plans for a railway similar to Railway No. 4 of the 1878 Session, to be built by either company, together with the doubling of the line between Caerphilly and Machen. Although powers for this line were granted under the PC&NR Act of 10th August, 1882, nothing further was done in the matter. On 7th May, 1884 a letter from Sir George Elliot was read to the B&MR traffic &

OPEN TO TRAFFIC

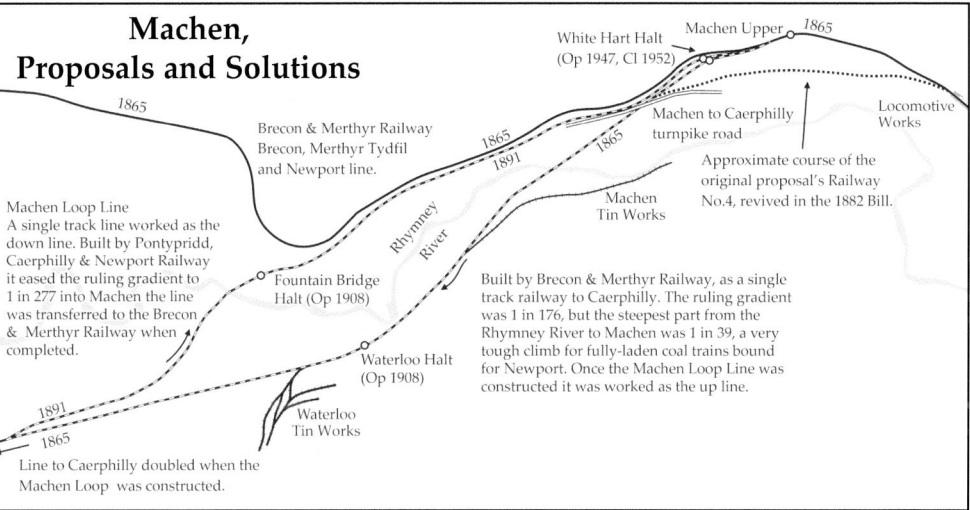

works committee suggesting that for the time being the Machen incline should be worked with additional haulage supplied by that company.

There the matter rested until April 1885. In that month Sir George Elliot suggested that if the B&MR undertook to make the authorised improvement at Machen, he would pay the company £6,000, or £8,000 if it also doubled the whole of the Caerphilly branch. This proposal floundered, however, when the estimate of the work required came in at £38,000, somewhat higher than Sir George had envisaged.

In the 1886 Parliamentary Session the PC&NR again sought to bring this issue to a head, with a proposal for a new avoiding line at Machen, together with the abandonment of the railway authorised by the Act of 1882. However, the resulting Bill was opposed by the Brecon & Merthyr Railway and was subsequently withdrawn. On 26th July, 1886 the B&MR's engineer recommended the construction of an avoiding line with a gradient no greater than 1 in 277, which would remove the need to double the Caerphilly branch. Although the B&MR's general manager was instructed to see Sir George Elliot and the landowners with this proposal, nothing more came of this idea.

Further evidence of the PC&NR's growing frustration with this lack of progress, at a time of increasing traffic, came in November 1886 when the company deposited fresh plans for an avoiding line. Once again the Bill, which also sought the abandonment of the 1882 line, was opposed by the B&MR. However, negotiations between the two companies produced an agreement, dated 9th May, 1887, and the subsequent withdrawal of the B&MR's petition against the PC&NR Bill. This agreement provided that upon its completion (assuming the Act was passed) the 'Machen Loop Line' would become the property of the B&MR, with the revenue from traffic between Caerphilly and Machen being divided equally between the two companies. Shortly after the signing of this agreement, the B&MR general manager was instructed to arrange for the purchase of land necessary for doubling the Caerphilly branch between its end-on junction with the Rhymney Railway at Van and the commencement of the Machen Loop Line.

The PC&NR Act received the Royal Assent on 8th August, 1887. In addition to authorising the construction of the Machen Loop Line (2 miles 3.80 chains) and the abandonment of the line authorised in 1882, this Act also sanctioned the creation of an extra £45,000 capital, together with borrowing powers for a further £15,000, with five years being allowed for completion of the works. The PC&NR was also empowered to enter into working and traffic agreements with the B&MR, with that of 9th May, 1887 being confirmed and scheduled to the Act. Lastly, an extension of time was granted for the completion of the Pontypridd-Penrhos Junction line as a passenger railway.

Work did not start on the new railway until the following Spring. On 27th April, 1888 the traffic & works committee of the B&MR heard that the PC&NR had commenced excavation near the Machen end of the line, and had applied for a junction and permanent way materials. This being agreed, it was left to the general manager to arrange terms. At Gwaun-y-Bara, at the opposite end of the loop line, a new junction in the single line was reported to be ready for Board of Trade inspection on 10th December.

Work progressed without undue hindrance, and on 24th September, 1890 the Brecon & Merthyr Railway general manager advised his traffic & works committee that the Machen Loop Line was nearing completion, and that the PC&NR had sought permission to work traffic over this line. On 1st November the first loaded coal train passed over the new railway, which was restricted to down mineral and goods traffic only. The old B&MR line continued to be used by both up and down trains, including all passenger workings. Conventional double line operation between Caerphilly and Machen depended upon the completion of the doubling of the short length of Rhymney line between Caerphilly and the end-on junction with the B&MR line, at Van. This was not ready for Board of Trade inspection until 22nd June, 1891, with the report by Major Marinden of 11th July recommending approval for the use of the new works.

With this link completed normal double line working could be effected between Caerphilly and Machen, with the Machen Loop Line becoming the down line and the old B&MR line the up. Board of Trade sanction was applied for on 19th August, 1891, the new line being expected to be ready for inspection on 24th of that month. In his report of inspection, dated 26th August, Colonel Rich stated:

> 'I have the honour to report for the information of the Board of Trade that in compliance with the instructions contained in your Minute of 21st inst, I have inspected the Machen Loop and the doubling from Caerphilly to Machen.
>
> The Machen Loop will form a down line from the junction with the Rhymney Railway near Caerphilly to Machen Junction and station on the B&MR, and this together with the doubling from Caerphilly will form a double line for the PC&NR Co. from Caerphilly to Machen, a distance of about 3½ miles. The Machen Loop is some distance from the old single line, which will now form the up line on this section of railway. The gauge is 4 ft 8½ inches. The permanent way consists of a Vignoles pattern rail, that weighs 72 lbs per yard. It is fished and fixed with fang bolts and clips to sleepers laid transversely 2 ft 8 inches apart, except those next to the rail joints, which are only 2 feet apart. The sleepers are 9 feet by 10 inches by 5 inches. The railway is ballasted with cinders and fenced with posts and rail and stone walls.
>
> The works consist of five overbridges that have stone abutments and wrought iron girders with brick arches between the iron transverse girders.
>
> Four underbridges all have stone abutments. Two consist of stone arches, one has wooden beams and the fourth has wrought iron girders that carry the railway.
>
> A viaduct over the Rhymney river consists of four spans of 45 ft 6 inches and 47 ft 6 inches. The abutments and piers are of stone and the tops are crossed with continuous wrought iron girders. These works are substantially built. The wrought iron girders are sufficiently strong by calculation and shewed moderate deflections when loaded.
>
> The colliery junction at Rhos Llantwit is worked from a raised cabin. The points and signals are interlocked. It contains 14 working levers.
>
> There are no stations on this new second line.

Colonel Rich, who appears to have been somewhat confused as to ownership, identified a number of minor defects, none of which were sufficiently important to stand in the way of Board of Trade approval. With this hurdle overcome, Machen Loop Line was opened to down passenger traffic, but without any formal ceremony, on 14th September, 1891.

Under the agreement of May 1887 the Machen Loop Line was to be transferred from the Pontypridd, Caerphilly & Newport Railway to the Brecon & Merthyr Railway upon completion. However, the date on which this transfer took place remains unclear. On 28th October, 1891 the B&MR engineer presented his traffic & works committee with an estimate of the cost of completing the line prior to taking it over from the PC&NR. The company's general manager suggested that a conveyance of the lands with plans defining boundaries should be called for, but the committee decided to seek the solicitor's advice on this issue. The B&MR solicitor, J. R. Cobb, did not consider such action to be necessary, but recommended that proofs of acquisition should be asked for, the general manager being instructed to carry this out on 4th November.

To complicate matters, the apportionment of tolls between the two companies, as provided for in the 1887 agreement, applied, in the case of goods and mineral traffic, from 1st November, 1890, and for passengers from 14th September, 1891, the opening dates in both cases. However, in practical terms the change of ownership was signalled by the withdrawal of the PC&NR's platelayers and others employed on the Machen Loop Line on 2nd November, 1892, the line then being left in the charge of the Brecon & Merthyr Railway engineer.

Little had been done to remove the other hindrance to the efficient working of through traffic over the Pontypridd-Caerphilly-Newport route. Under its agreement with the Pontypridd, Caerphilly & Newport Railway of August 1881, the Rhymney Co. was under an obligation to provide a second line of rails between Penrhos Junction and Caerphilly

Having just crossed Fountain Bridge viaduct, the major structure on the Machen Loop Line, one of the surviving Pontypridd-Newport limited-stop trains runs past the halt of the same name on 30th August, 1956. Only down trains called at this halt.

D. K. Jones

West Junction, when this became necessary for the conduct of the traffic. However, the latter company showed a marked reluctance to commit itself to such expenditure. The matter was raised by the Pontypridd, Caerphilly & Newport Railway in January 1887, but the Rhymney directors took the view that no 'public necessity' existed for this work. Notice requiring the doubling to be carried out was served in the Spring of 1888, but the Rhymney Co. still refused to act, and it was not until 1906 that a second line of rails became available on this section.

Taking Stock

By the end of 1891 the various sections of the PC&NR, completing the new route between Pontypridd and Alexandra Dock, were all in place and carrying traffic. This then is an appropriate point at which to pause and take stock of other developments which had occurred in the district since the passing of the PC&NR Act in 1878.

The 1880s had been a momentous decade for railway promotion in South Wales, with the convergence of rapidly growing coal output and restricted railway and dock facilities providing the incentive for a number of new schemes. By far the most important of these was the Barry Dock & Railways, incorporated in 1884 and opened five years later. Somewhat less successful was the attempt to tap the traffic of the Rhondda Fawr from the west by means of the Rhondda & Swansea Bay Railway (R&SBR), incorporated in 1882 and opened in stages between 1885 and 1895. Meanwhile, the Marquess of Bute had finally constructed the contentious Roath Dock, which was opened on 24th August, 1887 and subsequently served by the Roath branch of the Taff Vale Railway (opened 23rd April, 1888). Other proposals had failed to get off the ground, however, the most noteworthy being the Ogmore Dock & Railway, which was formally abandoned in 1891.

The effects of all this promotional activity were equally significant. The Taff Vale Railway had lost a substantial tonnage to the Barry line, which had undercut its rates on coal traffic. As a result, there were unsuccessful attempts to bring about the 'fusion' of the TVR and the Bute Docks in 1888 and 1889, while on 2nd September, 1889, in an act of sheer desperation, the Taff Vale Railway reduced its coal rate by about 22½ per cent in a vain attempt to head off the Barry challenge. This was followed, in May 1891, by a revolt of the TVR's shareholders and the appointment of an entirely new board of directors and chairman, following the resignation en masse of their predecessors.

In terms of traffic, by the end of the decade Barry was shipping over 3 million tons of coal a year, with Cardiff experiencing a slight loss, and Penarth Dock having lost half its trade. In comparison with that of the Barry Dock & Railways, the traffic attracted to Alexandra Dock, via the PC&NR, was relatively modest, amounting to just over 363,000 tons in 1890.

The PC&NR had also attracted attention from other quarters. Its broadly east-west alignment made it an eligible candidate in the long-running search for a suitable alternative route with which to challenge the GWR's monopoly between London and South Wales. Towards the end of 1882 plans were deposited for the West of England & South Wales Railway, from the authorised Swindon & Cheltenham Extension Railway (later part of the Midland & South Western Junction Railway), via Nailsworth, the Severn Bridge, Lydney and Newport to a junction with the B&MR at Bassaleg, from where running powers would give access to Cardiff and the TVR system. This proposal was reported to have been 'postponed' in January 1883.

Dissatisfaction with the GWR continued in spite of the opening of the Severn Tunnel in 1886, although, given that the route to London was then still via Bath, this is perhaps understandable. On 3rd September, 1892, the *Railway Times* noted that the South Wales papers had been full of reports of a new line between London and South Wales, making use of the PC&NR, TVR and Rhondda & Swansea Bay Railway. A conference of interested parties, held in Cardiff on 21st September, 1893, favoured a route via the PC&NR, Chepstow (with a bridge over the Severn) and Bath, to join the London & South Western Railway at Andover.

Finally, in November 1895 various leading lights in the Barry Railway Co. promoted the London & South Wales Railway, which was to run from the Barry Railway at Cogan to the capital, via Oxford. Powers were also sought for a junction between this line and the Brecon & Merthyr Railway, and to enter into working and traffic agreements with the PC&NR. However, when the GWR countered with its Bill for the 'Badminton Cut-off' between Patchway and Wootton Bassett, the Barry camp soon sued for peace. The GWR's direct line was authorised by its Act of 7th August, 1896 and opened to passengers on 1st July, 1903.

The 1880s had also seen the start of work on a second dock on Lord Tredegar's land at Newport. The first sod of the new 'South Dock' (authorised in August 1882 and constructed to the design of W. Stafford Smyth CE) was cut by Sir George Elliot on 30th January, 1883. The new dock was opened on 6th June, 1893, the Alexandra Dock & Railway board meeting adjourning for the occasion. The sluice gates were formally opened by Lord Tredegar and Sir George Elliot, the first vessel to enter the new dock being the S.S. *Hornby Grange*. By this date the original dock was handling over 3,600 vessels a year, the total trade amounting just over 3¼ millions tons, of which 86 per cent was coal. The South Dock was 20 acres in extent, measuring 1,500 feet by 640 feet, with an average depth of 30 feet. It was connected to the North Dock, as the original dock was now called, by means of a junction canal 65 feet wide.

Final Years of Independence

In spite of its close working relationship with the Alexandra Dock & Railway, and the presence of certain individuals on both boards of directors, the PC&NR was, for most of its independent existence, very much the personal domain of Sir George Elliot. No better illustration of this can be found than in 1893 when Sir George entered into negotiations with the GWR for the sale of the PC&NR. These were conducted in private, but word leaked out, the *Railway Times* of 18th November, 1893 noting that 'It is asserted that the GWR Co. is in negotiation for the purchase of the PC&NR.' However, the talks soon stalled. Sir George had sought a price equivalent to the total capital expenditure (just over £270,100) incurred by the PC&NR, but of this nearly £75,000 could not be accounted for. The GWR was not happy with this disparity, and also disliked the agreement with the TVR, together with a traffic arrangement with the Penarth Dock Co., which it felt was of an 'onerous character'.

Things came to a complete halt towards the end of 1893 when Sir George Elliot fell ill, having caught a chill at a political meeting in Cardiff. His son, G. W. Elliot, attempted to keep the negotiations going, but to no avail. Meanwhile, Sir George's condition had deteriorated, the initial affliction having developed into pneumonia, and on 23rd December, 1893 he died at the age of 78. He was buried on 28th December in the Hillside cemetery at Houghton-le-Spring, near Sunderland. In addition to his long and varied career as an engineer, manager and entrepreneur, he had sat in Parliament from 1868 to 1892, having represented the Monmouth constituency from 1886. With Sir George's passing nothing further was heard concerning the purchase of the Pontypridd, Caerphilly & Newport Railway by the GWR.

On 16th January, 1894, less than a month after Sir George Elliot's death, the surviving directors met to consider the future of the Pontypridd, Caerphilly & Newport Railway. The outcome was an instruction to Alfred Henshaw, the traffic manager, to bring forward a full report on the undertaking. Henshaw's report of 6th February, 1894 stressed the difficulties faced by the passenger train service, which incurred substantial costs in tolls for passing over the rails of four other companies, together with rent for the use of Pontypridd, Caerphilly and Newport stations. The mineral traffic had grown rapidly to reach just over 600,000 tons in 1887, but had then fallen back following the decision of the Powell Duffryn Co. to reduce the quantity of coal sent to Newport. This traffic had returned in 1893 following a fresh agreement with the colliery company which had given it very favourable treatment at Alexandra Docks. In addition, revenue had suffered following the opening of Barry Dock and the subsequent 'rate war'.

Henshaw also stressed the importance of the PC&NR to the well-being of the Alexandra Docks. The railway not only brought down coal from the Rhondda and Cynon Valleys, but also secured a much larger quantity of Monmouthshire coal to Newport for blending purposes. Without the PC&NR much of this Monmouthshire coal could be lost to Cardiff. Henshaw was clearly unhappy with the terms on which the TVR worked the traffic of the railway, describing them as 'favourable to that company'. However, this dissatisfaction did not extend as far as recommending severing the link with the TVR, the PC&NR board

Pontypridd (TVR) station looking north, with the extension to the down platform, including the bay for use by the PC&NR, nearing completion to the right of the picture in 1888. Two TVR 'Standard' 0-6-0 engines are featured, one in the goods yard on the right and the other on the down main line. *Author's collection*

having already decided, on 8th December, 1893, not to terminate the working agreement of June 1884. Lack of locomotive power was clearly a key consideration in this decision. On 5th June, 1893 the B&MR board had reluctantly declined a request from the PC&NR for the loan or hire of engines for working the coal traffic of its line, the directors noting, somewhat apologetically, 'that we have none to spare'. In these circumstances the PC&NR directors had little alternative but to accept the TVR's proposals for an extension of the working arrangements for a further 10 years from 1st October, 1895, which they did on 19th November, the new agreement being dated 30th December of that year.

On 1st May, 1894 Alfred Henshaw, having resigned as traffic manager of the Brecon & Merthyr Railway, a post he had held since 1863, took up his new position as the first general manager of the Alexandra Docks & Railway Co. He also assumed this role in connection with the PC&NR, where he had previously been designated 'Traffic Manager'.

The Pontypridd, Caerphilly & Newport Railway was soon faced with the need to commit significant resources to maintain its independent route between Bassaleg and Alexandra Docks. A timber viaduct on this line had quickly fallen into disrepair, its condition first being brought to the attention of the company's directors on 18th July, 1894, when it was agreed to spend £250 to keep it in a safe working condition for the following 6 months. Further repairs were required towards the end of that year, and on 19th November, 1895 the PC&NR board agreed to proceed with the construction of a deviation line to avoid the weakened structure. This was authorised by the AD&R Act of 7th August, 1896. Work started on 8th February, 1897, with it being reported on 7th April that opening was expected to take place on 12th of that month.

The mid-1890s saw a fresh outbreak of competitive frenzy in the narrow confines of the Taff Valley to the north of Pontypridd. The winning of coal at Dowlais-Cardiff Colliery, Abercynon in 1895 encouraged the Rhymney Railway to make a second attempt at an extension northwards from the PC&NR at Glyntaff. The 1896 Parliamentary Session also saw a Taff Vale Railway Bill for a continuation of that company's Pont Shon Norton branch north from Cilfynydd to join its Llancaiach branch, together with a short spur aimed at providing an alternative route to the new colliery. The Rhymney Bill was rejected by the House of Lords Committee, but its TVR counterpart fared better, receiving the Royal Assent on 7th August, 1896. This Act also authorised the provision of a short length of railway between the Pont Shon Norton branch and the PC&NR immediately to the east of the Taff Viaduct, which would have enabled TVR passenger trains from Nelson and Cilfynydd (introduced on 1st June, 1900) to reach Pontypridd station via PC&NR Junction, thereby avoiding that station's congested northern approaches. However, no attempt was made to build this line, although the powers for its construction were extended repeatedly through to 1915.

The death of Sir George Elliot in 1893 had removed a major reason for the continued independent existence of the PC&NR, and paved the way for its absorption by the AD&R Co. On 15th January, 1895 the AD&R board was informed that negotiations were in progress between Lord Tredegar and the executors of Sir George Elliot to enable their company to acquire the PC&NR, and for the resolution of various other outstanding matters. It was agreed, in principle, to seek powers to sanction any agreements reached, a Parliamentary Notice to this effect being published on 18th November. However, by the time of the AD&R board meeting on 21st July, 1896 a more cautious mood had taken hold. Whilst still supporting the principle of amalgamation, the directors decided that it would be better not to proceed with the Bill that Session.

By the autumn of 1896 things looked more certain, and on 18th September the Alexandra Docks & Railway board resolved to proceed with an amalgamation Bill in the ensuing Session. The resulting Act, which received Royal Assent on 6th August, 1897, authorised the transfer of the PC&NR to the AD&R Co. and confirmed three agreements which were scheduled to it. One of these, dated 12th April, 1897, between the AD&R Co., the Newport (Alexandra) Dock Co. and Lord Tredegar, covered the surrender of the lease of the AD&R by the Newport (Alexandra) Dock Co. on 31st December of that year, together with the release of property to the AD&R Co. Another, also dated 12th April, 1897, dealt with the transfer of the PC&NR to the AD&R Co., which was also to be effective from 31st December, together with the resolution of various issues still in dispute between the PC&NR Co. and Lord Tredegar.

One company which stood to suffer from such an arrangement was the Taff Vale Railway, and on 19th November, 1896 a Parliamentary Notice was published for a Bill seeking running powers for it over the PC&NR, the Tredegar Park Mile Railway and the GWR lines between Bassaleg Junction and High Street station, Newport. However, only those over the PC&NR survived the passage through the House to be included in the TVR Act of 6th August, 1897, which also had scheduled to it the agreements with the PC&NR of 1884 and 1895.

Thus on 31st December, 1897, after a life of just under 20 years, the PC&NR ceased to exist as an independent concern and became a railway adjunct to what was still primarily a dock company.

Chapter Five

Under the Alexandra (Newport & South Wales) Docks & Railway

Amalgamation of the Pontypridd, Caerphilly & Newport Railway with the Alexandra Docks & Railway Co. brought the two systems under the control of a single board of directors, chaired by Lord Tredegar, with Alfred Henshaw as general manager. However, as far as the former PC&NR line was concerned operations continued much as before: the TVR still supplied the locomotives and crew and worked the mineral trains, with the agreement of 30th December, 1895 still having just under 8 years to run; while the passenger trains continued to be hauled by AD&R engines, with the same ex-PC&NR carriages now forming part of the dock company's stock. Nevertheless, this seemingly settled picture was somewhat illusory as in the longer-term the arrangements for working the mineral traffic would need to be resolved, while considerable uncertainty surrounded the future of the unremunerative passenger service.

Although the PC&NR route between Bassaleg and Mendalgief Sidings, opened in 1886, provided additional capacity between Bassaleg and Alexandra Docks, it could not be reached from the Western Valleys Line of the GWR. Traffic from the Sirhowy and Western Valleys to Newport had continued to grow and on 3rd December, 1895 the GWR served notice on Lord Tredegar requiring him to provide two additional lines of rails over the Tredegar Park Mile, in accordance with the agreements of 1875 and 1883. Construction had started in 1896, with the new works being reported to be ready for inspection on 9th September, 1899 and were approved by Colonel Yorke for the Board of Trade on 8th November. Just over £5,500 was contributed towards the cost of this work by the PC&NR, prior to its absorption by the AD&R. There were then six lines of railway between Bassaleg Junction and the outskirts of Newport. The additional lines provided for the GWR became the up and down main and were used for passenger traffic, while the earlier ones were redesignated as the Relief Lines. The widened section northwards from Bassaleg Junction to Pontymister Junction was brought into use in 1901.

Passenger Service

Despite connecting three substantial population centres and loading quite well (considering the somewhat limited timetable), the Pontypridd-Caerphilly-Newport passenger trains consistently ran at a loss. Passing over the metals of four other companies and making use of three major stations, they incurred substantial costs in tolls and rent. In addition, as the PC&NR had only ever owned four coaches, non-availability, for whatever reason, brought with it the expense of hiring in substitute vehicles.

As early as November 1895 the Taff Vale Railway had offered to take over the working of the passenger trains, but this had been rejected by the PC&NR. Instead, the PC&NR board decided, on 19th May, 1896, to give notice to the TVR, GWR and B&MR of its intention to withdraw the service. Further fruitless negotiations took place with the TVR, against the background of that company's application to Parliament for running powers between Pontypridd and Newport. Discussions with the GWR proved more positive, however, and on 17th May, 1897 the PC&NR directors agreed to grant running powers to the GWR, statutory authority being provided by the AD&R Act of 6th August of that year, and to accept that company's offer for working the passenger traffic between Pontypridd, Caerphilly and Newport.

Glyntaff station features strongly in the foreground of this general view of Treforest, c.1910. Two of the AD&R's Barnum & Bailey coaches are in the yard, together with the ex-Mersey Railway coaches acquired in 1904. The Glamorganshire Canal passed close to the station, while to the extreme left of the view in the distance is Pontypridd Urban District Council's electricity generating station which adjoined the Council's gas works and tramway depot. *Ian L Wright collection*

With its absorption of the Pontypridd, Caerphilly & Newport Railway in December 1897, responsibility fell to the Alexandra Docks & Railway Co. for the transfer of the passenger service to the GWR. The TVR was not prepared to give up without a fight, however, and in the 1898 Parliamentary Session it applied for powers for construction of a railway of just under a mile in length from the Bassaleg-Alexandra Dock line to a passenger terminus of its own on the western side of Herbert Street, near its junction with Clytha Crescent, in Newport, together with the running powers applied for unsuccessfully a year earlier. This proposal attracted considerable support in the town, including that of the town council, this only being equalled by the disappointment felt when the Bill's abandonment was announced in April 1898.

On 5th October, 1898 the TVR board was informed that the AD&R Co. intended to cease working the Pontypridd-Caerphilly-Newport passenger trains and that the GWR proposed to continue the same. However, it was not until the following December that a public announcement of the GWR takeover was made. On 20th December the TVR agreed to the GWR making use of Pontypridd station in place of the AD&R. The agreement between the AD&R and the GWR was dated Saturday, 31st December, 1898, the transfer being effective the next day. However, as there was no Sunday service, the last day of AD&R operation was the Saturday, GWR working commencing on the following Monday morning, 2nd January, 1899. This development was reported to the AD&R board on 17th January, the directors being informed that the new arrangement was working satisfactorily.

In August 1900 John Macaulay, formerly traffic manager of the Mersey Railway, took up his duties as the new general manager of the AD&R following the death of Alfred Henshaw earlier in the year.

Motor Cars

Although the district between Pontypridd and Caerphilly had remained relatively sparsely populated, there were still requests for the provision of intermediate stations. Matters were not helped by a similar lack of facilities on the TVR, where there no stations between Treforest and Walnut Tree Bridge (as Walnut Tree Junction had become in 1886). In 1891 the PC&NR Co. built a station at Glyntaff, but this was not opened to passenger traffic. In December 1895 serious consideration was given to providing a station at Nantgarw, but this was ruled out because of cost. The early years of the 20th century saw further requests, with one

Alexandra (Newport & South Wales) Docks & Railway Motor Car No. 1.
Author's collection

for Groeswen being rejected in January 1901, followed by Rhydyfelin in October 1902.

In addition to the limited traffic prospects, any extra stops would have reduced the attractiveness of the through service, which provided a reasonably fast link between the coalfield valleys and Newport, as well as connections to and from London trains. However, the development of self-contained steam railcars (or 'Motor Cars' as they were generally known in South Wales) after 1900 offered hope of a low-cost solution to the provision of passenger facilities for the district concerned.

In November 1902 two of these vehicles were ordered by the London and South Western and London, Brighton & South Coast Railways Joint Committee for use on the Fratton-East Southsea branch. Car No. 1, which had been designed by Dugald Drummond, was completed in April 1903 and embarked on a series of trial runs. Later that month the car was loaned to the GWR for experimental use between Stroud and Chalford, in Gloucestershire, where it made its first run on 10th May,

1903. The success of these trials can be judged by the fact that the GWR subsequently introduced no less than 99 steam railcars.

The LSWR car also attracted attention in South Wales, especially from the TVR and the AD&R. The TVR, having previously toyed with the idea of an electrically-powered car, commenced work on their Car No. 1 in June 1903, it being completed during the following October. The AD&R was also quick off the mark, a rather cryptic board minute of 28th April, 1903 stating 'Motor Car – proposed purchase – to stand over'. On 9th May a committee of AD&R directors recommended the purchase of a car for use between Pontypridd and Caerphilly for which purpose plans, specifications and estimates were to be obtained. This was followed, on 26th May, by a decision by the AD&R board to acquire one of these vehicles at an estimated cost of £500, clearly a substantial underestimate, as the price of the company's first car was four times this sum.

Board of Trade approval was required for the introduction of the steam railcar and the somewhat novel arrangements associated with such a service. The AD&R's proposals were set out in a letter to the Board of Trade, dated 15th June, 1903. This noted that public representations had been made, from time to time, for an improved service between Pontypridd and Caerphilly, and that the company now wished to introduce a frequent Motor Car service with stops at close intervals between a terminal station at Pontypridd and the Rhymney Railway station in Caerphilly.

A meeting took place between officers of the Board of Trade and the Alexandra Docks & Railway Co. in August 1903, at which the former insisted that the driver should be at the leading end of the car at all times, suggesting the rather impractical use of turntables or reversing triangles to achieve this objective. The company's response of 1st September noted that the question of triangles had been looked into, but was 'out of the question upon physical and economic grounds'. Instead, it was proposed to duplicate starting, reversing, whistle and brake controls at the coach end of the car, with the driver always being at its leading end and the coach end always pointing downhill (ie towards Pontypridd). It was envisaged that the fireman would be a 'competent man', who would also act as conductor. While the Board of Trade was content with the proposed control arrangements, it was not prepared to accept a two-man crew, insisting that a driver, fireman and conductor should be employed. Also not to its liking were the folding steps proposed for use at the ground level halts; however, here the Board of Trade came up with a suggestion which pleased the railway company – fixed steps with a hinged flap to be added to the car.

With these matters settled, the AD&R board, at its meeting on 16th February, 1904, authorised the purchase of a car from the Glasgow Railway Engineering Co. of Govan, at an estimated cost of £2,000. Accommodation for the car was approved on 26th April, and on 28th June an agreement to be entered into with the Rhymney Co. for the use of that company's line from Penrhos Junction, together with its Caerphilly station, was endorsed by the AD&R directors. However, no attempt appears to have been made to make similar use of the TVR's Pontypridd station, even though the AD&R, as successor to the PC&NR, enjoyed the necessary running powers. Congestion at that station, coupled with the additional rent and tolls that would have been payable, were probably the deciding factors. Instead, the new service was to terminate at a separate station on the former PC&NR line immediately to the east of the bridge over Tramroad (so named because it had formed the route of Dr Richard Griffith's Tramroad from Trehafod) and about 500 yards by road to the south-east of the main entrance to the TVR station. The GWR passenger trains would not be affected by these proposals and were to continue to run between the TVR station at Pontypridd and Newport, without stopping west of Caerphilly.

On 24th August, 1904 the AD&R informed the Board of Trade that the new car had arrived at Newport, and that it and the eight ground level halts (usually but somewhat misleadingly referred to as 'stations' by the AD&R) between Pontypridd and Caerphilly were ready for inspection. This was conducted by Colonel E. Druitt on 31st August, his report, completed the following day, stating:

> I have the honour to report for the information of the Board of Trade that in compliance with the instructions contained in your Minute of 25th August, I have inspected the arrangements made for a Motor Car service between Pontypridd and Caerphilly on the Alexandra (Newport & South Wales) Railway.
>
> This portion of the line is about 6¼ miles in length and the gradients are easy.
>
> At Pontypridd, Glyntaff, Treforest, Rhydyfelin, Dynea, Upper Boat, Groeswen and Nantgarw ground platforms have been provided for both up and down trains (at Pontypridd only one platform has been provided... ...They are railed off by barriers from the footpath approaches, and the barriers will be opened by the Conductors on the arrival of the cars. At Upper Boat a foot overbridge has been provided to save passengers crossing the line to reach the down platform. At Rhydyfelin an occupation crossing is used for the down platform.
>
> At Pontypridd it is not desired to run the car into the Taff Vale station, like the ordinary trains, so the cars stop at the new ground platform on the up line

to Pontypridd and then run back on the same line a distance of 400 yards to the PC&N Interchange Sidings Signal Box, and reach the down line through a crossover road opposite the signal box...

All the new platforms are provided with a lamp at the entrance barrier.

A shelter has been provided at the Pontypridd Platform.

Having described certain features of the car, Colonel Druitt concluded:

The company have attended very well to all the details to make the arrangements described above safe and convenient, and I can recommend the Board of Trade to sanction their use for Motor Car services for passengers.

Board of Trade approval was conveyed to the AD&R on 5th September, 1904, but the service had already commenced on the first day of the month.

Alexandra (Newport & South Wales) Docks & Railway Motor Car No. 2.

Author's collection

The new Motor Car service appears to have been much appreciated in the district and was soon pronounced a success by the AD&R; at the half-yearly meeting of the company's shareholders on 23rd February, 1905, the chairman announced that:

> The number of passengers carried in the 4 months to December 31st was 53,869, and the number of miles run 10,196. The results of the working had been most satisfactory, and the service had proved a great local convenience, creating a new passenger traffic between stopping places not hitherto served.

Other developments were also attributed to this successful initiative: on 24th January, 1905 the AD&R board was informed that as a result of the establishment of the Motor Car service, twelve houses were being built at Rhydyfelin, a number were under construction elsewhere in the neighbourhood, and a further large number were contemplated.

A more frequent Motor Car service was soon felt to be necessary, and on 23rd May, 1905 the AD&R board approved the purchase of a second car from the same supplier, but at the increased cost of £3,000. The board also authorised the construction of a raised platform and extended booking office accommodation at the Tram Road station at Pontypridd. The improved service was introduced on 1st May, 1906, by which date the platform and improved facilities at the terminus had been completed.

The years following the introduction of the Motor Car service between Pontypridd and Caerphilly saw a number of similar developments on other lines in the area. On 12th March, 1906 the GWR put on a car between Merthyr and Newport, running via Quakers Yard, Hengoed, Risca, and Bassaleg. However, one company was unwilling to play a direct role in the railcar revolution. The B&MR's attitude was made clear by its chairman at the half-yearly meeting of that company's shareholders on 15th August, 1906, the record stating:

> In reply to a Shareholder, who asked why the Company could not put on Motor Cars like the Taff, Great Western and other companies, the Chairman said such cars would not suit, as they had to work with the Cambrian and Midland Cos. It was to their interest to work as cheaply and as safely as they possibly could. There was the question of capital. If shareholders would say where the capital was to be got, they would be happy to use it for the benefit of the line.

However, this reluctance on the part of the B&MR did not prevent it accepting an offer from another company to operate such a service over part of its system. On 19th February, 1908 the B&MR board agreed a proposal from the Rhymney Co. for the provision of a Motor Car service between Caerphilly and Machen. The Rhymney had been something of a latecomer to the Motor Car scene, with an invitation to tender for construction of its two cars having been agreed by its board on 2nd November, 1906. Cars replaced trains on its Aber branch, between Caerphilly and Senghenydd, on 1st October, 1907, the Machen route being operated in conjunction with this service from 1st April, 1908.

Halts were provided at Gwerndomen, Waterloo (up trains only) and Fountain Bridge (down trains only) between Caerphilly and Machen. However, the exact date of their opening remains unclear: a Rhymney Railway notice announcing the commencement of the Caerphilly-Machen service and the opening of halts elsewhere makes no mention of them, although they do appear as a footnote in Bradshaw for October 1908. A later but somewhat short-lived halt was that at White Hart, near Machen, which was opened on 12th May, 1947 and closed on 30th June, 1952.

Another local Motor Car service which might have appeared to be directly competitive with that offered by the AD&R was introduced by the Cardiff Railway Co. on 1st March, 1911 between Rhydyfelin Platform and Cardiff (Rhymney) station. Although the Cardiff Railway cars served much the same district between Rhydyfelin and Nantgarw, with their stopping places rather better located than those of the AD&R, the two services tended to serve different markets. The Cardiff Railway cars provided a direct link with Cardiff (for such a journey, via the AD&R, passengers would have needed to travel via Caerphilly), but did not run through to the important centre of Pontypridd, so competition was, in practice, somewhat limited.

Tramway and Bus Links

Passengers between Pontypridd and Newport could, for many years, make use of street tramways at each end of their journeys. At the Pontypridd end an electric system opened between Treforest, Pontypridd and Cilfynydd on 5th March, 1905. The tram depot was located alongside the gas works in Treforest, the route itself competing with that of the Alexandra Docks & Railway Motor Car service between there and Pontypridd. However, as the trams ran past the Tram Road station, they also enabled passengers arriving by the Alexandra Docks & Railway cars to continue their journeys into the heart of the town. Looking ahead, this tramway was superseded by a trolley bus route in 1931, which was itself abandoned on 31st January, 1957.

At Newport a horse-drawn tramway had been promoted from High Street station to Pillgwenlly, via Commercial Street and Commercial Road, in 1872. At the inquiry into this proposal, on 13th March, 1873, Mr T. Dyne Steel, engineer to the scheme, asserted that if, when the Alexandra Dock opened, communication with the centre of Newport was not good, then there would be a risk of a new settlement developing at the dock, to the detriment of the old town. The tram route was opened on 1st February, 1875, providing the first link in what was to become an extensive network. Electric power was introduced between High Street station and Pillgwenlly on 9th April, 1903, and the service was extended from the southern terminus along Alexandra Road to the Dock Gates on 3rd December, 1917. Closure came on 6th September, 1937.

In addition to operating one of the first steam railcar services in South Wales, the AD&R was also in the forefront of motor bus development. On 1st January, 1906, the company started running buses between the Pillgwenlly tram terminus and the Pier Head, with some journeys being extended to High Street (GWR) station. Statutory authority for this enterprise was obtained under the AD&R Act of 1906. With the extension of the tramway to the Dock Gates in 1917, the bus service was confined to the Docks area, eventually being withdrawn in 1933.

Mineral Traffic

It is clear that from late 1903, when the Alexandra Docks & Railway started accumulating a stock of locomotives suitable for main line operation, that the company had no intention of renewing the working agreement with the Taff Vale Railway when it expired. On 28th March, 1905, the AD&R board was informed that this arrangement was due to terminate on 30th September of that year, and approved a notice to that effect, to be served on the TVR. The deadline in question was subsequently extended, first to 31st October, 1905, and finally to 30th April, 1906. In the event, the TVR proved somewhat reluctant to give up working the AD&R traffic. Renewal terms were suggested by its general manager, Ammon Beasley, this being accompanied by a thinly veiled threat, made on 13th August, 1905, that the TVR would 'unquestionably' exercise its running powers over the AD&R, as contained in its Act of 1897, in the event of the agreement being terminated.

The AD&R board was not impressed by either the entreaties or the sabre-rattling, however, and continued to develop its plans for taking over the working of the Pontypridd-Alexandra Docks mineral trains.

A '56XX' 0-6-2T No. 6642 runs on to the PC&NR-built Machen Loop Line at Gwaun-y-Bara with a down mineral train on 4th October, 1957.   D. K. Jones

Such a change required substantially improved facilities for the transfer of traffic from the TVR at Pontypridd, and, on 24th October, 1905, approval was given to the enlargement of the Interchange Sidings, together with the erection of two new signal boxes, at an estimated cost of £11,681 2s. 4d. The new works were notified as ready for inspection on 19th April, 1906 and were the subject of a favourable report to the Board of Trade by Lt. Colonel E. Druitt on 28th April.

The last day of Taff Vale Railway operation was Monday, 30th April, 1906, the Alexandra Docks & Railway taking over the working the following day. From then on mineral traffic from the TVR was either worked direct to the Interchange Sidings, or tripped there from Coke Ovens sidings on the Rhondda branch to the west of Pontypridd, the AD&R then working block coal trains through to Mendalgief Sidings at Alexandra Docks with its own engines and crews. Additional accommodation was also necessary at the Newport end, with the expenditure of just over £7,000 on extra sidings and a water tank, between Park Yard and Cardiff Road, being authorised on 16th November.

During this period the AD&R also sought to emphasise its railway credentials by including, in its Bills in the 1904 and 1906 Parliamentary Sessions, applications for powers to change its name to the 'Newport and South Wales Railway', but both attempts ended in failure.

Later Schemes

Apart from the Bassaleg-Mendalgief Sidings line, with its connection with the Brecon & Merthyr Railway at Bassaleg, the export coal trade of the Alexandra Docks remained wholly dependent on the GWR for access to the docks lines. Between 1906 and the outbreak of the First World War, the AD&R put forward a number of proposals aimed at bridging the gap between its line and the LNWR at Nine Mile Point, thereby avoiding the need for Sirhowy Valley traffic to pass over GWR metals. The first attempt was rejected by Parliament in 1907, but a second scheme, which also added a branch to Risca, proved more successful, receiving the Royal Assent on 18th August, 1911. A revised scheme was authorised by the AD&R Act of 7th August, 1914, but the war years soon put paid to any thoughts of further railway expansion.

From the early 1880s through to the First World War numerous proposals were put forward for a direct rail link between the Monmouthshire Valleys and the port of Cardiff. No less than five attempts were made between 1883 and 1888 to promote the Cardiff & Monmouthshire Valleys Railway in a variety of forms (the last being under the auspices of the Monmouthshire Lines Bill of the TVR), while in later years schemes were put forward by the Rhymney, Barry, Cardiff, GWR, B&MR and LNWR companies. The only practical results of all this legislative activity were two short spurs constructed by the GWR, which linked the upper part of the Sirhowy Valley with the Rhymney Railway; these were Hengoed-Ystrad Mynach (opened 13th November, 1893), and Tredegar Junction-Bird-in-Hand Junction (on 30th November, 1893). Also built by the GWR was the Western Loop at Newport (opened on 6th April, 1886), which enabled trains from the Western Valleys Line to reach Cardiff, without the need for reversal at Newport.

Perhaps the most threatening of all these schemes was that proposed by the Barry Railway involving an extension from its line at Penrhos to the LNWR at Nine Mile Point and the Western Valleys Line of the GWR, near Cross Keys. Authorised on 28th August, 1907, this enactment proved to be something of a Pyrrhic victory, as a clause in the Act required the rates charged per ton per mile to be the same whether the traffic was destined for Newport, Cardiff, Penarth or Barry Docks, thereby denying the Barry Co. its usual tactic of undercutting the rates charged by its rivals. Had this line been built, which the offending clause and the First World War combined to prevent, then substantial quantities of coal from the Monmouthshire Valleys could well have been diverted away from Newport, seriously harming the prosperity of the Alexandra Docks.

Years up to the Grouping

The decade up to the outbreak of the First World War saw substantial increases in both the capacity available and the volume of traffic handled at the Alexandra Docks. The new dock works involved a 48 acre extension to the South Dock (authorised by the AD&R Act of 15th August, 1904) and a new lock entrance (powers for which were contained in the company's Act of 4th August, 1906). The dock extension was opened in November 1907, practically doubling the area of the docks. The new lock entrance was opened on 14th July, 1914 by HRH Prince Arthur of Connaught, and was 1,000 feet long by 100 feet wide, equipped with the most up-to-date coal tipping appliances. Prince Arthur had arrived from Avonmouth aboard Lord Tredegar's yacht *Liberty*. The GWR laid on a special train to bring guests down from Paddington, the train consisting of nine first class bogie carriages and no less than six restaurant cars, hauled by 'Star' class 4-6-0 No. 4040 *Queen Boadicea*. The dining cars were detached at Alexandra Dock Junction, an AD&R engine working the remainder of the train over the docks lines to a temporary platform near the new lock entrance. For other less exalted

Coal tipping aparatus loading a ship in Alexandra Dock.   *Oakwood Press*

attendees arriving by train, including those from Pontypridd and Caerphilly, the arrangements were somewhat less convenient, given the distance of High Street station from the docks.

Great credit for the completion of these new works was attributed to the AD&R's former general manager John Macaulay, who had retired in 1913. His successor from 1st March of that year was J. H. Vickery, latterly assistant to the general manager of the LSWR.

Godfrey Morgan, the first Viscount Tredegar and formerly chairman of the AD&R Co. had died on 11th March, 1913, before seeing this great work come to fruition. His title of Baron Tredegar passed to his nephew, Courteney Morgan (1867-1934), but the viscountancy (which could only pass from father to son) lapsed. Courteney Morgan was created first Viscount Tredegar (second creation) in 1926.

In common with other South Wales lines, the upturn in traffic over the former Pontypridd, Caerpilly & Newport Railway line was most pronounced in the years immediately before the outbreak of war. The average quantity of coal conveyed during these years was 1.5 million tons per annum, compared with the 0.75 million tons recorded in 1905. This represented about a quarter of the coal exported from Newport Docks, the total peaking at just under 6 million tons in 1913.

Following the declaration of war on 4th August, 1914, the Government took control of the nation's railways under powers contained in the Regulation of the Forces Act 1871. Responsibility for

Alexandra Docks & Railway Co. locomotive No. 26.   *Author's collection*

management was vested in the Railway Executive Committee (REC), comprising the President of the Board of Trade and the general managers of the principal railway companies.

For the railways the war years were characterised by loss of men and materials to the services, increased traffic generally and special workings related to the war effort, coupled with rising costs and reduced maintenance. On 9th December, 1916, in an attempt to reconcile these conflicting pressures, the REC wrote to the individual companies setting out proposals aimed at curtailing passenger train mileage and releasing men and materials for the armed forces, and, in particular, seeking the raising of fares, the reduction of services, and, where possible, the closure of lines and stations. In response, the GWR withdrew its Pontypridd-Caerphilly-Newport through service (together with the Merthyr-Hengoed-Newport railcars) from Monday, 1st January, 1917, arrangements being made for the AD&R local service to be extended from Caerphilly to Machen from the same date. As there was no Sunday service the last GWR trains ran on 30th December, 1916. A further wartime economy measure, involving the 'pooling' of open wagons, was introduced on 2nd January, 1917, the AD&R falling within the GWR group for the purposes of this arrangement.

Another development during the war years was the introduction of a unified system of management covering the Taff Vale, Rhymney and Cardiff Railways, under an agreement between the three companies of 6th July, 1917. The AD&R was not directly affected by this arrangement, but this merging of the Cardiff dock and railway interests would, in more normal times, have caused considerable alarm in Newport, and was clearly a significant pointer to the post-war era.

A considerable traffic in steam coal was worked during the war years from the valleys served by the TVR to Scotland, principally to Grangemouth for transfer to the fleet at Scapa Flow. The route employed, via Quakers Yard and Pontypool Road, became increasingly congested, and on 27th March, 1918 the TVR traffic committee was informed that arrangements had been made for a proportion of this coal to be taken via the former PC&NR and Rhymney lines to Hengoed for transfer to the GWR. In addition, a somewhat smaller flow passed from South Wales to Southampton and Gosport, via the Severn Tunnel.

As part of the war effort a factory was opened at Alexandra Docks to repair shell cases and cartridge boxes retrieved from the battlefields. This facility – the 'National Box Repair Factory' – was built on a substantial scale, occupying 13 acres near the lock entrance. To provide transport for the munitions workers an extension of Newport Tramways was opened from Pillgwenlly to the Dock Gates on 3rd December, 1917. A special train service was then laid on to transfer the workers from the Dock Gates to the South Quay. The factory was later purchased by the GWR from the War Department, under an agreement of 21st November, 1924.

Government control of the railways was extended for a further two years in 1919. It came to an end on 15th August, 1921, four days before the passing of the Railways Act 1921, which grouped the various independent companies into four large concerns. In advance of these developments, the *GWR Magazine* of October 1920 had announced the creation of a 'New relief route' between Newport and Neath, via the Pontypridd, Caerphilly & Newport, Taff Vale and Rhondda & Swansea Bay Railway lines. However, apart from the introduction of a summer Newport-Treherbert-Aberystwyth passenger service in August 1920 and the continuation of certain through freight workings over the former PC&NR line, there appears to have been little of substance to this announcement.

Under the Railways Act of 19th August, 1921, the Alexandra Docks & Railway became a 'constituent' of the enlarged Great Western Railway. This higher status was clearly a reflection of the scale of the docks undertaking, rather than any pretensions on the railway side. Indeed, the AD&R had the distinction of having the smallest railway route mileage of the 28 'constituent' companies named in the Act. Amalgamation took place on 25th March, 1922, when the Government-appointed Railway Amalgamation Tribunal approved the financial settlement between the GWR and the AD&R Co., but with all matters being back-dated to 1st January of that year. The day before approval was granted by the Tribunal a party of very senior GWR officers – W. W. Grierson (chief engineer), R. H. Nicholls (superintendent of the line), E. Lowther (chief goods manager) and C. B. Collett (chief mechanical engineer) – made a highly symbolic tour of inspection of the docks at Newport, before going on, the following day, to visit those at Cardiff, Penarth and Barry.

Chapter Six

Grouping to Closure

Great Western Years

The first significant changes to affect the former PC&NR lines, following the amalgamation of the Alexandra Docks & Railway with the Great Western Railway, were organisational ones. On 8th May, 1922 the GWR established a new Cardiff Valleys Division, taking in the lines of the former Taff Vale, Rhymney, Barry, Cardiff and AD&R companies. This structure proved rather short-lived, however, as in October 1924 the new division was abolished, with most of its lines, including those between Pontypridd and Caerphilly, being transferred to an enlarged and reshaped Cardiff Division. The Caerphilly-Machen-Newport section, on the other hand, went to the newly created Newport Division.

The Alexandra Docks were brought within the control of the new Docks Department of the GWR, with J. H. Vickery, the last general manager of the AD&R, being appointed as the company's first chief docks manager. However, Vickery did not hold this post for very long, retiring in the early part of 1924 to be succeeded (for an equally short tenure) by Edward Lowther, the GWR's chief goods manager and formerly general manager of the Port Talbot Railway & Docks Co.

The change of ownership meant that the practice of terminating trains from Machen and Caerphilly at the Tram Road station in Pontypridd became an obsolete and unnecessary inconvenience for passengers. This station was therefore closed on 10th July, 1922, with its trains then being admitted to the vastness of the ex-Taff Vale Railway station, and in particular to the Newport and Caerphilly bay, which had been vacated on the withdrawal of the Great Western Railway-worked Pontypridd-Caerphilly-Newport service in 1917.

Unified ownership also brought with it other changes. On 1st July, 1924 the 'stations' on the 'Caerphilly and Pontypridd Line' (as it was known to the GWR) acquired the more appropriate designation of 'Halt', with Rhydyfelin and Nantgarw also receiving the suffix 'High level' to distinguish them from their ex-Cardiff Railway counterparts. At the same time, the ex-TVR station at Pontypridd became 'Central' to distinguish it from the former Barry Railway station at 'Graig'.

Although the Grouping had brought the two sections of former PC&NR line between Bassaleg and Alexandra Docks within the ownership of the GWR, one anomaly that it did not address was the intervening Tredegar Park Mile Railway, which still remained the property of Lord Tredegar (ie Courtenay Morgan). The GWR now possessed running powers and paid tolls in respect of its traffic on three sets of running lines through Tredegar Park, the southernmost pair having been used by the AD&R. In 1913 the tolls paid had amounted to £17,402 in the case of the GWR and £1,878 for the AD&R. This question was brought to the attention of the GWR board by the company's general manager, Felix Pole, on 14th February, 1923. Having heard that negotiations had taken place for the acquisition of the TPMR, the directors ordered that this should be proceeded with, but at a cost not exceeding £365,000. On 16th March it was reported that a price of £360,000 had been agreed, with purchase being effective from 1st January of that year. The transfer was subsequently confirmed by an agreement between the GWR and Lord Tredegar, dated 14th December, 1923.

The period immediately after the Grouping coincided with a short-lived boom for the coal industry of South Wales. When this faded towards the end of 1924, the output of this important coal-producing district began the long decline from which it was never to recover. By 1939 coal production of the Rhondda Valleys had fallen to less than a third of that achieved in the peak year of 1913. A number of factors were behind this precipitous trend: post-war reparations; loss of foreign

The AD&R 'station' at Rhydyfelin at about the time of the Grouping, with a Pontypridd (Tram Road)-Machen train arriving. The train comprises 0-4-2T No,14, ex-Motor Car No. 2 and a Barnum & Bailey coach. An up mineral train has just passed en route for Interchange Sidings.
P. Rutherford

markets following the restoration of the gold standard in 1925 and the long-term trend for the world's shipping to substitute oil for coal as fuel; and the effects of the General Strike and longer miners' strike of 1926. By the time of the world wide economic collapse in 1931, the area was already acutely depressed, with many mines closing and output at others curtailed. For the railways, including the former Pontypridd, Caerphilly & Newport Railway lines, the result was a substantial loss of traffic and a consequent reduction in the number of train movements.

The decline of the export coal trade of Newport docks was just as rapid, falling from about 7 million tons in 1923 to only about a third of this total by 1934. Part of this loss can be attributed to the general recession affecting the South Wales coal trade, but there were other special factors at work. Newport's advantage over Cardiff in terms of the 'free on board' price had been removed by the District Coal Committee. There was also a growing tendency for Monmouthshire coal to be taken to Cardiff for blending purposes before being despatched. Previously such coal either had been shipped unmixed, or had been blended at Newport, the latter being of particular importance to the traffic of the former PC&NR lines. The result again was fewer coal trains passing over these lines to the docks at Newport.

Passenger traffic, particularly over shorter distances, also fell away during the 1920s, partly as a consequence of the general recession, but mainly in the face of rapidly growing bus competition. As early as 2nd August, 1917 the urban district councils of Caerphilly (CUDC) and Bedwas and Machen (B&MUDC) had obtained Acts of Parliament empowering them to operate buses along specified routes. In the case of CUDC this covered roads from Senghenydd to Caerphilly and Caerphilly to Bedwas Bridge, while the B&MUDC Act referred to the section of the main Caerphilly-Newport road lying within the council's administrative area, together with its continuation to the centre of Caerphilly, subject to the consent of CUDC. B&MUDC ran a Caerphilly-Machen service, while a private operator, J. Beavis of Risca, introduced a Machen-Newport service in July 1923.

By 1928 the CUDC bus undertaking was being run at a loss, leading to unsuccessful negotiations for its acquisition by the GWR. However, agreement was reached for the operation of a joint service between Caerphilly and Newport, although the GWR interest ended with the formation of the Western Welsh Omnibus Co., under an agreement of 27th March, 1929, which led to the merger of the bus operations of the railway company with those of South Wales Commercial Motors Ltd. The new company, which came into being on 1st April of that year, operated the Caerphilly-Newport service under a working agreement with CUDC. In 1935 Western Welsh took over the Machen-Newport route operated by J. Beavis (by then trading as the Danygraig Omnibus Service), when it absorbed that concern.

Municipal enterprise was also a force to be reckoned with on the Pontypridd-Caerphilly section. On 28th July, 1930 Pontypridd Urban District Council (PUDC) introduced a bus service between that town and Rhydyfelin. This was followed by the development of a Pontypridd-Caerphilly route, jointly operated with CUDC. Also of significance for journeys to Pontypridd was the frequent Pontypridd-Cardiff bus service which had been introduced by the Rhondda Tramways Co. (renamed the Rhondda Transport Co. in June 1934) in March 1924 and a similar service operated by Cardiff Corporation from 1928.

The local trains between Pontypridd and Caerphilly were especially vulnerable to bus competition because many of the settlements they purported to serve were some distance from the halts, and far better related to the main road through the Taff Valley. Unfortunately, ticket sales for halts between Pontypridd and Caerphilly were not recorded individually, but were grouped with those of the main stations. Nevertheless, it is clear from other stations in the vicinity that the decline in patronage must have been very substantial. For example, between 1922 and 1932 ticket sales at Church Village and Llantwit stations on the nearby Pontypridd-Llantrisant line fell by nearly 90 per cent, largely as a result of intense bus competition.

In spite of this onslaught, the Pontypridd-Caerphilly-Machen local trains continued much as before. Indeed, there was even some new investment. On 14th May, 1928 the old ground level halt at Rhydyfelin was replaced by a new raised facility, some 16 chains nearer Caerphilly. The new arrangements were inspected by Lt. Colonel A. H. L. Mount, on behalf of the Minister of Transport, on 3rd November, 1928. The reverse occurred in the case of the halts on the ex-B&MR section between Caerphilly and Machen where, from 26th June, 1929, the original timber platforms were replaced by the ground level variety, similar to those found on the former PC&NR.

There was, nevertheless, one casualty during this period as far as the Pontypridd-Caerphilly section was concerned. Latterly few trains had called at Glyntaff Halt, which was poorly located and quite close to Treforest Halt, so its closure on 5th May, 1930 was not surprising. Also withdrawn, on 20th July, 1931, was the ex-Cardiff Railway service between Rhydyfelin and Coryton Halts, leaving the ex-PC&NR halts at Rhydyfelin, Upper Boat and Nantgarw alone to face the bus competition.

The inter-war period saw improvements to the capacity of the multi-track section between Bassaleg and Newport. In 1925, the old single line connection at Bassaleg between the ex-B&MR line and the former PC&NR route to Alexandra Docks (referred to as the 'Alexandra Dock Line' by the GWR) was replaced by a new double junction. This was followed, on 11th April, 1926, by the bringing into use of a new scissors crossover between the Alexandra Dock Line and the Relief Lines at Park Junction. Finally, on 11th December, 1939 a new double junction was opened between the Relief Lines and the Alexandra Dock Line at Bassaleg Junction. These changes enabled the section between Bassaleg Junction and Park Junction to be worked as three pairs of double lines, catering for all movements between the various running lines.

The war years brought with them a reduced passenger service between Pontypridd and Newport, with the through trains to and from Merthyr being withdrawn for good from 25th September, 1939. However, wartime travel needs coupled with petrol rationing and fewer buses led to greater use of the trains, in spite of the restricted timetable.

On the freight side the war brought increased demand for coal, with the Pontypridd-Caerphilly-Newport route providing a useful bypass to the heavily populated urban concentration at Cardiff. Even so, the railway was still liable to disruption, as when a number of unexploded bombs discovered near Machen blocked the former B&MR main line and the down line between Caerphilly and Machen from 27th February to 1st March, 1940, when they were reopened for goods traffic. The blockade was re-imposed the following day to allow the bombs to be exploded. This resulted in some damage to the permanent way which necessitated single line working over the Caerphilly-Machen section until normal double line working was restored on 3rd March.

One other wartime development of note was the movement of USA Army locomotives from Newport to storage areas at Penrhos Junction and the former Barry main line north of Tonteg Junction, in the latter case passing over the full length of the former PC&NR between Caerphilly and Pontypridd.

The end of hostilities in 1945 left the railways in a similar state to that which had existed in 1918. They had been worked to the limit in the national interest, while maintenance had suffered as a result of wartime restrictions and shortages. This time, however, with a Labour Government elected in 1945, the response to the problem was wholesale nationalisation. This was effected by the Transport Act 1947, and from 1st January, 1948 the former PC&NR lines became part of the Western Region of British Railways.

British Railways Era

Nationalisation brought few immediate changes to the former PC&NR lines. The Pontypridd-Caerphilly-Machen-Newport passenger service was not affected by the spate of temporary closures which took place during the fuel crisis in the early part of 1951. However, on 2nd February, 1953, Rhydyfelin, the only halt between Pontypridd and Caerphilly with raised platforms, was closed, the last train having called on the previous Saturday, 31st January. In its latter years this halt had taken on an increasingly decrepit appearance and closure appears to have been brought about by the dangerous state of the platforms.

On 21st September, 1953, after much careful research and planning, a regular interval passenger service timetable was introduced between Treherbert/Merthyr, Pontypridd, Cardiff and Barry. However, no attempt was made to produce a similar pattern between Pontypridd, Caerphilly and Machen, something that did not auger well for the line's future. The resulting half-hourly service between Pontypridd and Cardiff enabled Newport to be reached from the Taff and Rhondda Valleys, via a change of trains at Cardiff, much more conveniently than by means of the former PC&NR line. Journeys via the latter route usually entailed an unwelcome wait for the connecting train at Machen, with its somewhat limited amenities.

The early 1950s saw an increasing number of passenger train withdrawals in South Wales, with Pontypridd losing two of its branch services in 1952, that to Llantrisant going on 31st March, followed by Ynysybwl on 28th July. There was then a pause, at least as far as Pontypridd was concerned. However, behind the scenes moves were afoot to continue this process of retrenchment. In April 1954 the Branch Lines Committee of the Western Region produced a report recommending the withdrawal of the Pontypridd-Caerphilly-Machen passenger trains. The report itself made depressing reading, finding that savings of about £9,000 would result from abandoning the service, including £2,803 accounted for by the train working staff of two drivers, two firemen and two passenger guards. Passenger receipts for the 12 months ending 31st December, 1952 had amounted to only £1,787 for a total of 47,160 journeys. Allowing for the transfer of some of the through traffic to the alternative route via Cardiff, it was estimated that the annual loss of income would only be £852.

Turning to alternative road services, the report noted that these comprised an hourly service between Caerphilly, Machen and Newport operated by Western Welsh and the Pontypridd-Caerphilly service, also

A Machen-bound auto-train, comprising an ex-Rhymney Railway carriage and ex-GWR driving car (at the rear) arrives at Groeswen Halt on 7th May, 1948. The distinctive signal box is visible behind the locomotive. *Ian L. Wright*

hourly, jointly worked by PUDC and CUDC, together with other more local services, principally in the vicinity of Pontypridd. For through rail passengers the route via Cardiff was considered to be a satisfactory substitute for that via Machen.

The report concluded:

> The line under review can be divided into two sections with varying characteristics.
> The section Machen Junction to Caerphilly serves a very sparse and scattered area and does not provide a sufficient traffic potential to ensure economic services.
> From Caerphilly to Pontypridd, however, the line passes through an industrialised area with housing estates in close proximity to the halts, and the traffic is heavier over this section.
> An examination of current bookings from Caerphilly to Pontypridd indicates an increase over the corresponding period of last year, which may be attributed to the fact that the experimental cheap return rail fare is 4*d.* cheaper than the road.
> Notwithstanding this favourable tendency, which might possibly be further developed to some extent, it is the view of the Committee that having regard to the small fares involved, sufficient revenue could not be secured to offset the

economies to be achieved by the withdrawal of the service, which, if fully quantified, would amount to approximately £9,000 per annum. To achieve parity with these economies, it would be necessary to increase passenger receipts by 500 per cent (or 450 per cent if the parcels traffic is included), which would appear to be an impossible achievement under the most favourable conditions.

The intermediate halts have no platforms or lighting and in some cases no shelter and consequently the withdrawal of the passenger train service would not effect any appreciable economy in respect of maintenance and renewal of station buildings etc.

Through freight services over the section are heavy and the withdrawal of the passenger train services would not enable any savings in respect of permanent way maintenance and renewal to be made.

In all the circumstances, and notwithstanding the recent improvement in bookings between Caerphilly and Pontypridd, the Committee recommend the complete withdrawal of passenger train service between Machen and Pontypridd, with the exception of one service in each direction between Newport and Caerphilly required in connection with the conveyance of staff employed at the Caerphilly Works.

Consultations took place with the Transport Users Consultative Committee, local authorities and the trades unions and in the Spring of 1956 it was announced that the trains between Pontypridd, Caerphilly and Machen were to be withdrawn at the start of the winter timetable. According to figures made public at the time, the average number of passengers then using this service each day was a meagre 28, rising to 64 on Saturdays, representing 1.4 and 2.9 passengers per train respectively.

As an aside, it is worth noting that on 31st March, 1955 the Western Region had produced a document, entitled 'Proposed Dieselisation of Cardiff Branch Passenger Services', which identified a list of services proposed to be diesel-operated. Three other routes (Bridgend-Nantymoel, Llantrisant-Penygraig and Pontypridd-Machen) had been considered, but as their futures were then under review they were omitted from the final proposals.

The closure date for the Pontypridd-Caerphilly-Machen service was fixed for 17th September, 1956, but as there was no Sunday service, the last trains ran on Saturday, 15th September. A wreath, bearing the inscription 'Evergreen memories from the station staff at Machen. R. I. P.', was attached to the train engine. The final train, the 10.00 pm (Saturdays only) from Machen to Pontypridd, was reported to have been 'almost packed' with railway enthusiasts and officials, the latter group including the Pontypridd station master Mr H. E. Merrett. With the end

The last passenger train 10.00 pm 17th September, 1956.   *Author's collection*

of the passenger train service the remaining halts at Treforest, Dynea, Upper Boat, Groeswen and Nantgarw were closed, together with those between Caerphilly and Machen.

Following the withdrawal of the passenger trains, the Pontypridd-Caerphilly-Machen line settled down to a freight only existence. By the 1950s coal traffic between the Rhondda Valleys and Newport Docks was but a shadow of its former volume. Symptomatic of this decline was the closure of the section of the Alexandra Dock Line between Dock Sidings and West Mendalgief, officially from 3rd September, 1959. As a result, any traffic for Alexandra Docks was worked via the ex-GWR section between Park Junction and Maesglas Junction. The remainder of the Alexandra Dock Line, between Bassaleg and Park Junction, was closed as a through route and converted into sidings on 20th October, 1963. By this date only a comparatively meagre coal traffic was handled at the docks, and what little there was ended in 1964 with the concentration of the residue of the trade at Barry and Swansea. Nevertheless, the Pontypridd-Caerphilly-Newport route continued to be used by trains passing to Newport, Severn Tunnel Junction and other destinations to the east of the town.

By the early 1960s this traffic was considered insufficient to justify the retention of double track between Pontypridd and Penrhos Junction, leading to the singling of this section on 28th January, 1962.

Passenger service withdrawals accelerated during the early 1960s in the era of 'piecemeal' closures, in the run-up to the publication of the Beeching Report in March 1963. The former Brecon & Merthyr Railway services between Brecon/New Tredegar and Newport were casualties of this period, both being withdrawn on 31st December, 1962. The line between Fleur-de-Lis and Bedwas was closed to all traffic from this date, the surviving section above Machen being singled on 15th August, 1965 and worked as a siding from 20th November, 1967. Unadvertised workmen's trains had continued to run between Newport and Caerphilly after the end of the Pontypridd-Caerphilly-Machen service in 1956, but these ceased on 1st July, 1963, following the closure of Caerphilly locomotive works

One closure brought extra business to the Pontypridd-Caerphilly-Newport route, albeit for a relatively short period. With the withdrawal of through freight trains between Aberdare and Pontypool Road, via Quakers Yard and Crumlin, on 11th April, 1964, this traffic was diverted via Pontypridd and Caerphilly, augmenting the existing flows over the former Pontypridd, Caerphilly & Newport Railway line.

Unfortunately, this additional traffic was not enough to prevent further erosion of the network. On 20th July, 1964 the section between Caerphilly and Machen was singled, resulting in the abandonment of the former down line (including the Machen Loop Line built by the PC&NR) and leaving the former up line (originally the Caerphilly branch of the B&MR), with its 1 in 39 climb approaching Machen, to suffice for all traffic passing between Caerphilly and Newport. This arrangement proved extremely short-lived, however, as on 28th July the former down line was re-instated at the expense of the former up line, which was then abandoned.

This period also saw substantial investment in modern signalling systems on the South Wales main line. Multiple aspect signalling was introduced in stages, with the area to the west of Newport, formerly controlled by Gaer Junction and Alexandra Dock Junction boxes, becoming operational on 26th November, 1962, albeit under temporary arrangements. The Newport power box was opened on 9th December, the scheme being completed on the incorporation of the Ebbw Junction area on 19th May, 1963. A similar facility at Cardiff was brought into use on 27th March, 1966, its area of control joining that of Newport at Marshfield and extending as far west as Llantrisant.

The net result of these changes was a considerable increase in the capacity of the four track main line between Cardiff and Severn Tunnel Junction. From Pontypridd it was, of course, downhill all the way to the South Wales main line, which was reached via Penarth North Curve, to the west of Cardiff station.

Compared with this greatly improved route, that involving the former Pontypridd, Caerphilly & Newport Railway line now offered few if any advantages. In particular, singling of the Pontypridd-Penrhos Junction and Caerphilly-Machen sections had greatly reduced its flexibility. Indeed, some traffic between the valleys to the north of Pontypridd and Newport was already being worked via Radyr and Penarth North Curve even before these changes had taken place. It was not unexpected, therefore, when on 2nd January, 1967 the former PC&NR line was closed between Glyntaff goods station and Penrhos Junction, through traffic between Pontypridd and Newport being diverted via Radyr and the South Wales main line. This was followed, on 1st May of that year, by the complete closure of the ex-Rhymney Railway line between Penrhos Junction and Caerphilly West Junction. The last remaining stub of the former Pontypridd, Caerphilly & Newport Railway, between Pontypridd and Glyntaff goods yard, did not last much longer, being closed on 31st July, 1967. The line between Caerphilly and Machen (part of which had been built by the PC&NR) was closed on 20th November of that year, the surviving trains being diverted via Penrhos Junction, Radyr and Penarth North Curve. The remaining portion of the former Brecon & Merthyr Railway line, between Bedwas and Bassaleg Junction, was worked as a single line siding from that date.

To complete this depressing catalogue of decline and degradation, coal traffic was diverted away from the former Rhymney line between Aber Junction and Walnut Tree Junction on 21st June, 1982 to run via Llanishen, initially 'on a trial basis', but was never to be restored. A final enthusiasts' excursion – the 'Rod Mill Rattler' – ran over this route on 23rd October, leaving this, the last of the many railways through Penrhos Junction, to be lifted by the middle of 1984.

In the east, the ex-Brecon & Merthyr Railway line between Bedwas and Machen Quarry was taken out of use after the final removal of wagons from Bedwas Colliery on 8th April, 1985, leaving the long siding serving Machen Quarry as the last surviving section of the former Brecon & Merthyr Railway in operation.

An auto-train leaving Groeswen Halt. *Author's collection*

Chapter Seven

Along the Lines

A passenger travelling from Pontypridd to Newport in pre-Grouping days would have passed over the lines of no less than five railway companies, including those of the Pontypridd, Caerphilly & Newport Railway or its successor, the Alexandra Docks & Railway. Thus, in order to provide a complete picture, it will be appropriate to give a brief outline of the sections owned by other companies, in addition to a more detailed description of the PC&NR itself. The resulting 'tour of inspection' takes place around the time of the Grouping in 1922, but with references to past and future developments at particular locations.

In common with other South Wales railway companies, including the TVR, Rhymney Railway and B&MR, the PC&NR adopted the local convention of 'up' being 'up the valley' and 'down' being 'down to the sea', the run from Pontypridd to Newport therefore being in the down direction. Distances are given in miles and chains and correspond with those employed by the GWR, being measured from Bassaleg Junction.

Pontypridd

When opened for freight only in 1884, the PC&NR joined a double line section of the Taff Vale Railway, just south of Pontypridd station, by means of a double junction ('PC&N Junction'), controlled by a signal cabin in the vee between the two lines. The station itself then consisted of platforms each side of the running lines, with a bay for Rhondda branch traffic on the up side. Improvements to accommodate the PC&NR passenger service were approved by the TVR board on 15th September, 1887, the tender of Mr Mathias, contractor of Porth, for £944 5s. 4d. being accepted on 5th November of that year. However, as these alterations were not ready in time for the commencement of the service on 28th December, the PC&NR train initially was allowed to use the main line platforms, possibly reversing via the triangular junction to the north of the station, as was the practice with Llantrisant and Cowbridge branch trains terminating at Pontypridd.

As part of these changes a replacement signal box, containing 30 working and the same number of spare levers, was constructed on the Pontypridd side and to the east of PC&N Junction, being reported on favourably by Colonel Rich for the Board of Trade on 25th January, 1888. A double junction was then laid in the PC&NR, leading from its main

A general view of Pontypridd (TVR) after the completion of the goods avoiding lines in 1902, but before the start of the rebuilding of the passenger station in 1907. The long down platform, together with the bay used by PC&NR trains, crosses the lower part of the picture. *C. W. Harris collection*

The rebuilt station at Pontypridd (TVR), the original view being postmarked September 1914. *Ryan collection, courtesy J. A. Peden*

line to a single bay line and a new platform face (known as the Newport and Caerphilly bay) on the down side of the station. A crossover provided a trailing connection from the bay line to the Taff Vale Railway down main. PC&NR trains were able to run directly to and from their bay platform, without making use of the TVR main line, while the bay could also be used for down TVR trains starting from Pontypridd.

This new layout, which was brought into use in May 1888, was the subject of a further report by Colonel Rich, dated 1st June. He was not happy with a number of features, particularly the width (only 6 feet) of the extended down platform over the High Street bridge, and the absence of any protection against the elements, and so was only prepared to recommend the granting of conditional sanction for the new works. In the event, it was not until 1894 that the bridge in question was widened, while the Newport and Caerphilly bay remained uncovered until the station was rebuilt.

The rebuilding of Pontypridd station spanned the period between the turn of the century and the outbreak of the First World War. The first stage involved the construction of two relief lines for mineral traffic on the up side of the passenger facilities. For a while the Newport and Caerphilly bay was only available for departures, but with the completion of the second relief line, reported to be ready for inspection on 17th October, 1901, a facing connection was provided from the TVR up main line to the bay line. Unfortunately, under this arrangement trains from Caerphilly had to cross the down main at PC&N Junction, then run over part of the up main, before re-crossing the down to reach the bay platform, a manoeuvre which could be awkward at busy times. Trains departing the bay platform did not enjoy an independent run on to the Caerphilly line, but had to share the down main to PC&N Junction.

Plans for the new passenger station were approved by the TVR in November 1905, construction commencing in earnest in October 1907. The new arrangements comprised a vast island platform with two inset bays and two short Motor Car bays at the up end, and a single bay for Caerphilly and Newport and other terminating trains at the down. The new Newport and Caerphilly bay was brought into use on 7th March, 1910, although the station rebuilding was not finally completed until 1915. The new arrangements were a considerable improvement on the temporary layout of 1901, but trains to and from Caerphilly still had to share the approaches to Pontypridd station with TVR main line trains.

One of the few features to survive this immense upheaval was the signal box at PC&N Junction, dating from 1888. This box was eventually closed during the weekend of 13th-16th June, 1970.

The former Newport and Caerphilly bay continued to be used by other trains for many years after the withdrawal of the Pontypridd-Caerphilly-Machen service in 1956, and was not finally taken out of use until 2nd November, 1980.

Pontypridd-Caerphilly

Almost immediately after parting company with that of the TVR, the PC&NR line passed over Broadway (formerly Tramroad), by means of a skew lattice girder bridge. This bridge was rebuilt with a plate girder span double that of the old in connection with a road widening scheme, completed in 1939. With the singling of the line in 1962, the short double track section from PC&N Junction ended just beyond this bridge.

On the up side of the line on the embankment just beyond this bridge, was Tram Road station (14 m. 41 ch.). Originally opened in May 1904 as a ground level affair, the improved arrangements, brought into use in May 1906, consisted of a single raised platform, 100 feet long, approached by a ramp up from the road. A crossover, which had been installed at this time just beyond the east end of this platform, avoided

Pontypridd (Tramroad) station, looking towards PC&N Junction c. 1922. Note that despite the station always being referred to as 'Tramroad' the nameboard only mentions 'Pontypridd'. The curvature at this place was such as to require the provision of check rails on both running lines. *H. J. P. Rutherford*

the need for cars to run 'wrong line' to Interchange Sidings, before gaining access to the down line. The line then crossed the River Taff by means of a viaduct of three lattice girder spans, resting on stone piers and abutments.

The entrance to the Interchange Sidings was immediately beyond the Taff Viaduct. Sidings were not provided at this point until 1888, and then only on the insistence of the Rhymney Co. In their original form they consisted of two sets of dead-end sidings on the down side, one served off the up line and the other off the down, with connections between the two. The entire layout was under the control of a centrally placed signal cabin, known as Interchange Sidings.

The new arrangements at Interchange Sidings, brought into use April, 1906, comprised six loop sidings on the down side. Direct access was provided from the down line at the Pontypridd end, with trailing connections to the running lines at both ends. A loop was also provided on the up side. The whole layout was controlled by two signal boxes: 'Interchange Sidings' (14 m. 36 ch.) and 'Glyntaff' (14 m. 6 ch.).

Two additional loop sidings were subsequently added on the up side of the line, both being reported to be ready for inspection on 27th March, 1908. By this date the signal boxes had been renamed 'Interchange Sidings West' and 'Interchange Sidings East' respectively. The west box was closed in 1941. The junctions with the up and down running lines at

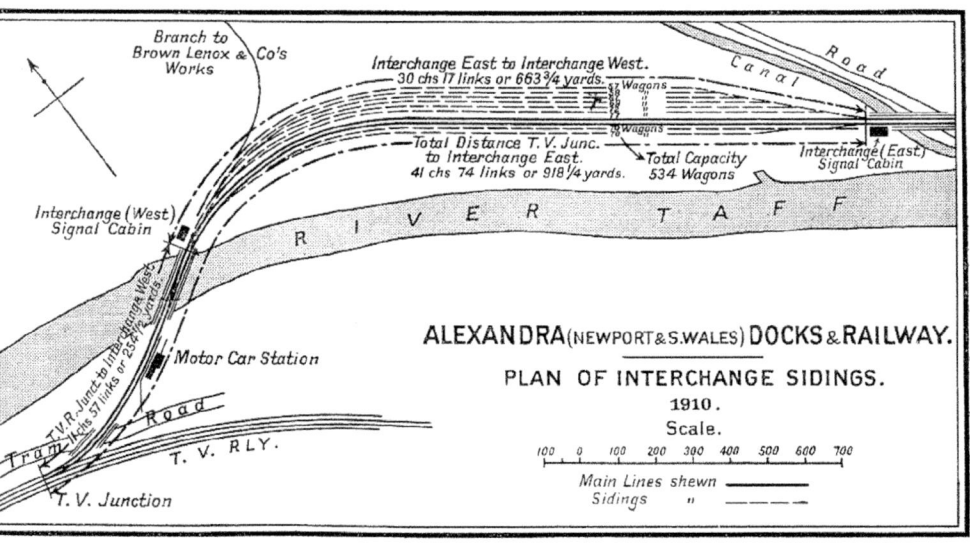

Interchange Sidings from the *Railway Gazette*, 21st April, 1911.

the west end of the sidings were removed, together with the loop lines on the up side. During the late 1940s the embankment at this place suffered from spontaneous combustion, causing a number of sidings to be taken out of use, with single line working being employed until the problem was overcome. Three more sidings were recovered in February 1953. Interchange Sidings East box was closed on 28th January, 1962 on the singling of the Pontypridd-Penrhos Junction line.

Near the western end of the Interchange Sidings a short spur ran off to serve the Newbridge chain works of Brown, Lenox & Co. This factory had been opened in 1818 by Captain Samuel Brown to produce chain cable for the naval and merchant fleets of the world, and had been served by two basins off the Glamorganshire Canal. No connection was ever made with the Taff Vale Railway, but that from the PC&NR had been laid by March 1895. A modified layout was approved by the AD&R board on 24th June, 1902, and the private siding agreement was eventually terminated on 29th July, 1967.

Just beyond the eastern end of Interchange Sidings the line crossed the Glamorganshire Canal and Pentre-Bach Road by means of what Colonel Rich, the Board of Trade inspector, described as a 'viaduct', but which was in fact two adjoining underbridges. Curving gently to the

A general view of Treforest, c.1910, provides some valuable details of Glyntaff station, with the up platform and building, goods shed and bridges over Pentre-bach Road and the Glamorganshire Canal in the foreground. *Author's collection*

south west, it then reached Glyntaff station (14 m. 0 ch.), complete with the only goods depot on the former PC&NR.

A quarry had been worked at Glyntaff during the construction of the PC&NR, providing stone for the Taff Viaduct and other bridges in the vicinity. At the time of Colonel Rich's inspection of the line in February 1887, this quarry was served by a siding off the down line, controlled by a nearby signal box. On the introduction of passenger trains over the PC&NR in December 1887, the locomotive and coaches for the service were stabled at Glyntaff, the former in a stone-built engine shed on the down side of the line close to the bridge over Pentre-Bach Road. The connection from the down line to this 'engine siding' (which also served the quarry) was moved a few yards nearer Caerphilly in 1889. There was also a trailing crossover between the running lines, near the signal box.

In February 1888 the PC&NR traffic manager, Alfred Henshaw, had recommended against the provision of any intermediate passenger stations between Pontypridd and Caerphilly. The company's minute book does not refer to this subject again until 30th August, 1890, when it was reported that:

> ...several memorials from the inhabitants of Pontypridd, Glyntaff and the neighbourhood were submitted to the meeting, the memorialists wishing the new passenger station to be situated near the cemetery instead of the Glyntaff Quarry.

This was followed, on 12th September, 1890, by a public meeting at the Libanus Chapel, Treforest for

> ...the purpose of appointing a deputation to wait upon the Directors of the PC&NR and urging them to revert to the original site selected for their proposed new station at Glyntaff.'

The PC&NR minute book is again silent on this development, but the company was clearly not receptive to the entreaties of the local residents as it proceeded to erect the new station at Glyntaff Quarry. Work started towards the end of 1890 and was completed about a year later, at a cost of £1,786 18s. 5d. The new station consisted of up and down platforms, each with a single-story building of timber construction, with the signal box at the back of the up platform at about its midpoint. However, having built this impressive facility at not insignificant cost the company then made no attempt whatsoever to open it to the public. No Board of Trade inspection is recorded and Glyntaff station did not make an appearance in the public timetable.

As might be imagined, this situation gave rise to much adverse comment in the locality. On 17th September, 1896 a petition from the inhabitants of Treforest was submitted to the meeting of Pontypridd Urban District Council asking for the council's influence to be brought to bear in persuading the PC&NR Co. to open its Glyntaff station for passenger and other traffic. The Council readily acceded to this request, which was reported to the railway company's board meeting the following day, although nothing more is recorded in the minute book.

Nevertheless, a reply to the Pontypridd Urban District Council was forthcoming, and is reported (by the *Pontypridd Observer*) to have given rise to the following exchange at the Council meeting on 15th October, 1896:

> ...a letter was submitted from the Manager of the PC&NR Co., which stated that, in answer to the Council's letter, the Directors do not see their way to erect a new station at Pontypridd.
> The Chairman: "There is nothing said about the opening of the old one?"
> The Clerk: "No, Sir."

Thus having failed to open the station at Glyntaff, the PC&NR board now seemed somewhat reluctant to acknowledge that one even existed! A further letter was despatched by the Pontypridd Urban District Council and reported to the PC&NR board on 15th December, 1896, but to no avail, and so Glyntaff station remained unopened.

A view of Glyntaff station from across the Glamorganshire Canal in the early years of the 20th century, showing, from left to right, the goods (formerly engine) shed, the unused up station building and the original signal box. *Stephen Rowson collection*

Just why this station was built and then not opened remains a mystery. It is possible that, given the unremunerative nature of the passenger service, the PC&NR Co. may have been reluctant to incur additional costs by staffing Glyntaff station. Also, in the circumstances, the company may have calculated that failure to open a station would provoke much less dissent than a proposal to close an existing one. Whatever the reason, this state of affairs persisted beyond the amalgamation of the PC&NR with the AD&R in 1897 and the takeover of the Pontypridd-Caerphilly-Newport passenger service by the GWR two years later.

Glyntaff Quarry had ceased production by 1898. However, on 20th November, 1900 the AD&R board approved an application for additional siding accommodation to serve the quarry, a private siding agreement with one John Gibbon being dated 26th February, 1903. It was also decided to open a depot for general goods traffic at this place. There was a delay while vehicular access and other matters were addressed, Glyntaff station eventually opening for goods traffic only on 2nd June, 1902. The works undertaken included the conversion of the old engine shed into a goods shed, the removal of the down passenger platform, and the provision of additional sidings. In AD&R days the goods shed was adorned with a substantial hoarding proclaiming the company's name in full in large letters above the even larger 'GLYNTAFF GOODS STATION'.

Glyntaff was selected as the centre of operations for the Motor Car service between Pontypridd (Tram Road) and Caerphilly, introduced in September 1904, the erection of a Motor Car shed being ordered on 26th April of that year. This shed, which was long enough to accommodate Motor Car No. 1, was built on the down side of the line, and was served by a short siding which ran back off one of the goods yard lines. Motor Cars called at Glyntaff from the start of the service, but it is not clear whether they made use of the old raised platform on the up side of the line as the Board of Trade inspection report refers to 'ground platforms' being present at all 'stations'. The arrangements for passengers on the down side also remain unclear, especially as the space between the running line and the goods shed siding was somewhat restricted.

With the purchase of a second Motor Car in 1905, additional accommodation was required at Glyntaff. Also, it was expected that as the original car shed was on the line of an intended branch of the Cardiff Railway (authorised by Act of 1897, but not built), it would need to be demolished. As a result, it was decided, on 23rd February, 1905, to erect a new shed capable of holding two cars, served by a short siding on the up side of the line. This work required a large amount of blasting to widen the rock cutting at this point, and also resulted in the shortening of the old up platform at its Caerphilly end.

The signal box was closed in 1906 in favour of a new box (known as 'Interchange Sidings East' from 1908), situated on the up side of the line immediately to the west of the canal bridge, and provided in connection with the enlargement of the Interchange Sidings.

On 22nd June, 1909 the AD&R board was informed that while engine No. 27 (an ex-GWR 0-6-0ST) was shunting a train of 45 empty wagons on the up line at Glyntaff, it had been turned into the second car shed road, instead of through the crossover onto the down line, and had collided with Car No. 1 and a trailer, damaging both vehicles and driving the latter through the end wall of the shed.

The original car shed was subsequently used for stabling locomotives, until it was closed in September 1922. The second shed was demolished in 1930, but the siding which had served it was not removed until 2nd February, 1947. Although Glyntaff Halt closed in May, 1930, the goods yard continued in use until 1967. The adjoining quarry, by then known as 'Pentrebach Quarry', was taken over by the Albion Coal Co., the private

Interchange Sidings (formerly East) signal box, Glyntaff viewed from the Pontypridd direction on 31st July, 1960. The turnout in the foreground then provided the only access to Interchange Sidings, while Glyntaff goods shed is visible just beyond the bridges under the line. *Michael Hale*

siding agreement being dated 16th February, 1924, but had ceased production by February 1925. The goods warehouse was without rail connection by 1926. On 13th December, 1934 the GWR's traffic committee agreed to recommend the expenditure of £2,000 on the construction of a large warehouse at Glyntaff for Messrs Elders & Fyffes Ltd, banana distributors. This was erected off the outer siding in the goods yard.

When the Pontypridd-Penrhos Junction section was singled in 1962 a short length of double line was retained from PC&N Junction, the single line commencing at the site of Tram Road station. The former down line was utilised to a point just beyond the site of Interchange Sidings West signal box, where it was slewed to join the old up line, which was then used throughout. A trailing crossover at Glyntaff was retained to give access to the goods yard, via a short section of the former down line. This line also served the remnants of the Interchange Sidings and the spur to the chain works. The connection to the running line was controlled by a ground frame (14m. 17ch.).

Leaving Glyntaff the line curved through a rock cutting, passing under a bridge carrying Glyntaff Road, to the halt at Treforest (13 m. 67 ch.). Only 16 chains from Glyntaff, Treforest was approached by pedestrian

On the last day, 15th September, 1956, of the Pontypridd-Machen service '64XX' 0-6-0PT No. 6411, bearing a commemorative wreath, rounds the curve to the east of Glyntaff, bound for Caerphilly and Machen. *D. K. Jones*

ramps down from the road bridge. Small waiting shelters were subsequently added on each side of the line.

The line then passed over Cemetery Road before curving to the east past Pontypridd Urban District Council's gas works, served by a siding (13 m. 57 ch.) which had been provided under an agreement between the Council and the PC&NR of 10th December, 1896. The gas works, which was on the up side of the line, had been formally opened by Mr Patrick Gowan, chairman of the Council's gas committee, on 9th September, 1896, but the siding serving it was not brought into use until 8th November, 1897.

In its original form this siding left the down line by means of a facing connection, with a single slip in the crossing providing a trailing connection to the up line. The layout was revised in 1908, being reported to be ready for inspection on 27th March, with a simple trailing connection off the up line and a trailing crossover between the running lines. A trailing siding was also added on the up side of the line. Lt. Colonel E. Druitt inspected the altered arrangements for the Board of Trade and recommended that approval be granted in his report of 9th April, 1908. A short loop siding was subsequently (by 1915) laid off the main siding to serve the electricity generating station which had been built by Pontypridd Urban District Council at the same time as the tramway to Pontypridd.

The down 'platform' and shelter at Treforest Halt, viewed from the south, 14th July, 1956.
R. M. Casserley

Treforest Halt looking towards Caerphilly, viewed from the bridge carrying Glyntaff Road over the railway.
L&GRP

A Pontypridd-Machen auto-train, hauled by '64XX' 0-6-0PT No. 6438, at Rhydyfelin Halt, 27th August, 1948. The first coach is former Rhymney Railway stock.
Ian L. Wright

The signal box was replaced by a ground frame under an agreement of 16th September, 1926, the crossover being removed at about the same time. The private siding agreement was terminated on 29th September, 1953, the connection and ground frame being taken out of use on 23rd May, 1954.

South of Gas Works Siding the line entered what in 1922 was still largely an unspoilt rural area. Following a sinuous course on the eastern side of the Taff Valley, it climbed at a constant gradient of 1 in 200 towards Penrhos Junction.

The original 'station' at Rhydyfelin (13 m. 17 ch.) was an extremely rudimentary affair, even by AD&R standards, with passengers gaining access to trains on either side of an occupation crossing, without any form of shelter. The later GWR halt, opened in 1928 and 16 chains nearer Caerphilly, was much more substantial, with raised platforms 100 feet long and a corrugated-iron 'pagoda' shelter on the up side to cater for the dominant flow of passengers towards Pontypridd. Both old and new halts were some distance from the rapidly-growing district of Rhydyfelin, which was much better served by the Cardiff Railway platform.

The line continued through mostly open countryside to Dynea (12 m. 55 ch.). The halt was situated on an embankment, on the Pontypridd side of an overbridge, with a timber-built shelter on the up platform, and originally served a small hamlet nearby. In October 1908 flooding of Dynea Brook resulted in the road under the railway being blocked with mud, and a breach in the Glamorganshire Canal bank between Dynea Lock and Maesaraul Bridge.

Dynea Halt, from a passing train, 14th July, 1956.   *R. M. Casserley*

Just beyond this halt was the site of the junction with the Dynea Colliery branch. Provided under a private siding agreement with the Dynea Colliery Co., dated 24th April, 1895, and reported to be ready for inspection on 1st August, the arrangements here consisted of trailing connections to both up and down lines, with a single slip in the down line crossing forming a trailing crossover between the running lines, all under the control of a signal box on the up side of the line. The siding agreement was transferred to J. L. Smith, owner of the renamed 'Dynea Llantwit Colliery', on 15th November, 1897, but the colliery did not last long under new ownership. It was abandoned on 30th June, 1899 the plant and materials being sold off on 6th February of the following year.

From Dynea the line continued its gradual ascent, passing through the woods of Fforest Newydd, to Upper Boat (11 m. 76 ch.). This halt was situated on the north side of an overbridge carrying a footpath which provided the only connection with the small settlement of Upper Boat, about ¼ mile to the south.

Beyond Upper Boat the line progressed along the hillside to Groeswen (11 m. 22 ch.), situated to the east of a bridge carrying the road from the village of Upper Boat to Groes-wen, about ¾ mile to the east. There was little in the way of settlement nearby, with the principal feature of interest being the remains of early tramroad feeders to the Glamorganshire Canal. When opened in 1904 the down platform consisted of planking laid between the rails of the colliery siding headshunt.

Groeswen station and signal box in AD&R days. Although somewhat crudely 'touched up', the photograph clearly showst that the down 'platform' has been laid between the rails of the headshunt and adjoining colliery siding. *Author's collection*

The 1887 Board of Trade inspection report on the PC&NR referred to a signal box and siding at 'Penygroes', a hamlet about ¼ mile to the north-east of the later Groeswen Halt. Groeswen Colliery, about 300 yards to the west of the main line and served by a short length of tramway via an inclined plane, had been opened in September 1893 by one H. D. Jones. It was taken over by William Turner & Co. in 1896. On 15th March, 1897 the Pontypridd, Caerphilly & Newport Railway seal was ordered to be affixed to a new siding agreement, the new owner being William Baker. This agreement was transferred to the Groeswen Colliery Co. from 6th December, 1898, and on 16th February, 1899, the AD&R board approved proposals for the reconstruction of the sidings and the provision of a new connection from the up line.

The new arrangements were brought into use on 14th August, 1899 under the provisional sanction of the Board of Trade, but final approval was withheld (in a report produced by Lt. Colonel Addison on 16th September) because of the poor view of the new connection from the signal box. After much protestation the AD&R agreed to relocate the box to the down side of the line, immediately south of the road overbridge. However, while this was ideal for the new connection, the view of the original points on the down side was not so good. As a result, the

Looking over the remains of Groeswen Halt, towards Caerphilly, from beneath the overbridge nearly two years after the last train had called, 10th July, 1958. The nameboard would not have survived so long in later years! *R. M. Casserley*

nearest set of points was removed, with the outer ones moved out and extra signals added. A single slip was also added in the crossing at the western end, forming a second crossover, and a new lever frame was provided in the signal box. The revised layout, which was reported to be complete and ready for re-inspection on 3rd December, 1901, was finally passed by Major Druitt of the Board of Trade on 31st January, 1902.

On 7th February, 1902 the colliery was sold to Groeswen & Caradog Collieries Ltd, the new private siding agreement being dated 28th October. This passed to the South Wales United Collieries (Groeswen & Caradog) Extension Ltd on 19th April, 1904, the colliery having changed hands about the middle of the previous year. An application from the new owners for an extension of the siding accommodation had been approved by the AD&R board on 1st December, 1903.

Groeswen Colliery was abandoned on 1st July, 1905. On 23rd January, 1912 the Alexandra Docks & Railway board agreed to affix the common seal of the company to an agreement with Frederick Bristow regarding traffic from Groeswen Quarry, but it is not known if any rail-borne business resulted. Groeswen siding had gone by July 1923.

A new down refuge siding was added to the north of the halt in 1908. The small timber-built signal box was later replaced by one of a larger non-standard design, the date of its frame being 1925. The down refuge siding was taken out of use on 21st January, 1949, with the remaining crossover following on 28th September, 1952.

Nantgarw (10 m. 32 ch.), the last stop before Caerphilly, was situated high above the village it was intended to serve, on the up side of the road to Caerphilly, again in a very sparsely populated area. Timber shelters were provided on both sides of the line under an instruction of 26th October, 1909. The line itself curved to the east at this point as it passed through a deep cutting to join the Rhymney Railway at Penrhos Junction.

Prior to the construction of the PC&NR all that existed at Penrhos was a simple single track junction between the Aber Junction-Walnut Tree Junction line and the Caerphilly branch of the Rhymney Railway. The PC&NR was double track from the outset, necessitating the doubling of short sections of the adjoining Rhymney lines and the provision of a double junction. A temporary siding was added off the down line of the PC&NR, close to the junction, in 1888.

The Rhymney branch of the Barry Railway from that company's main line at Tynycaeau Junction, opened on 1st August, 1901, joined the Rhymney line at Penrhos South Junction, that with the former PC&NR line then becoming Penrhos North. The Barry Co.'s B&MR branch,

'64XX' No. 6438 arrives at Nantgarw Halt with a Pontypridd-Machen auto-train on 22nd April, 1955. The cheap fares promotion which helped push up passenger numbers in the final years of the service is clearly advertised. *Ian L. Wright*

Penrhos South Junction with the signal box added by the GWR in 1935 on 6th September, 1956. A mixed freight is approaching the junction on the former Barry lines from Cadoxton, via Tynycaeau Junction. The centre line is the former Rhymney Railway line from Walnut Tree Junction, while on the right of the picture is the former PC&NR line, with a Pontypridd-bound single coach auto-train in the distance. The disused piers and abutments once carried the ex-Barry Railway Brecon & Merthyr branch over the other six lines of railway. *D. K. Jones*

opened on 2nd January, 1905, left the Tynycaeau Junction-Penrhos South Junction line at Penrhos Lower Junction, then climbed to cross the three sets of double lines – Barry, Rhymney and AD&R – by means of a plate girder bridge of three spans resting on brick abutments and piers.

In anticipation of extra traffic resulting from the opening of the Barry line to Penrhos Junction, the Rhymney board, on 10th February, 1899, had authorised the doubling of the section between Aber Junction and Penrhos Junction at an estimated cost of £2,700-£3,000.

With the growth of traffic on the PC&NR, the single line of the Rhymney Railway's Caerphilly branch, to the east of Penrhos Junction, became an increasingly irksome bottleneck. However, it was not until 8th April, 1904 that the Rhymney board approved a scheme for doubling this section, together with the construction of the Beddau Loop. The completed works were inspected for the Board of Trade by Lt. Colonel Druitt, his report being dated 20th October, 1906. The following year an exchange siding for the Rhymney Co.'s traffic was provided on the former PC&NR line on the site of the temporary siding of 1888. It was not until 12th February, 1928, however, that, as a result of increased coal traffic between Aber Junction and the former Taff Vale Railway main line, a second line of rails was brought into use on the former Rhymney Railway line between Penrhos Junction and Walnut Tree Junction.

A Machen-Pontypridd runs on to former PC&NR metals at Penrhos on 6th September, 1956. The siding on the far left was provided in 1907 for Rhymney Railway interchange traffic (being ready for inspection on 3rd June) but was laid on the site of an earlier temporary siding. *D. K. Jones*

Provision of a new centrally-placed signal box adjoining Penrhos South Junction was approved by the GWR traffic committee on 26th April, 1934, at an estimated cost of £4,385. The new 'Penrhos Junction' box replaced the old north and south boxes at this place.

From the high point in 1922 there followed a progressive reduction in the network of lines radiating from Penrhos Junction. The first to go was the former Barry B&MR branch, an early victim of post-Grouping rationalisation, which was abandoned by Act of 4th August, 1926. Through traffic was withdrawn from the former Barry Railway Rhymney branch following the destruction by fire of the signal box at Tynycaeau Junction on 31st March, 1963. The last surviving section of this line, from Penrhos South Junction to a dolomite quarry immediately to the west of Taff's Well viaduct, was closed on 14th December, 1967.

With the singling of the Pontypridd-Penrhos Junction section in 1962 the junction at its eastern extremity was also simplified. The former double junction gave way to a facing connection in the down line to Walnut Tree Junction, with access to the up line to Aber Junction provided by a single slip which had been retained from the earlier layout. The closure of the former PC&NR and Caerphilly lines in 1967 left only the Aber Junction-Walnut Tree Junction line in use, until it too was abandoned in 1982.

Watford Crossing signal box on the former Rhymney line between Penrhos Junction and Caerphilly West Junction on 30th July, 1960. The junction with the line from Aber Junction is visible in the distance. *Michael Hale*

The Rhymney line between Penrhos Junction and Caerphilly West Junction was about a mile long, and at the Grouping passed between the built-up area of the town and Caerphilly Common to the south. There was an intermediate signal box at Watford Crossing, which controlled the junction with the Beddau Loop from Aber Junction. This box, which replaced an earlier one on the opposite side of the line, was some 250 yards to the east of this junction, adjoining the level crossing which gave it its name.

Caerphilly

The Caerphilly branch joined the Rhymney main line at Caerphilly West Junction, originally by means of facing points off the up line, but with the addition of a second line of rails on the branch a double junction was laid in. The junction itself was controlled by a signal box on the north side of the line. The main line then continued through Caerphilly station which, prior to rebuilding, consisted of up and down platforms, with the goods yard adjoining on the north side of the line.

There was also an additional up platform, to the west of the bridge carrying the Cardiff Road over the railway, accessed by means of a

Caerphilly station *c.* 1905, before rebuilding started, looking towards Pontypridd. The splitting distant signals at the end of the up platform were for Caerphilly West Junction where Pontypridd trains turned off the Rhymney main line. *Lens of Sutton*

separate footpath down from this road. According to G. A. Sekon (otherwise Nokes), writing in the *Railway Magazine* in March 1907, GWR trains running from Newport to Pontypridd called at this platform rather than at the main one on the up side. Immediately beyond the station, at Caerphilly East Junction, the branch to Machen parted company with the main line and curved away to the north.

On 10th March, 1908 the Rhymney and Barry companies entered into an agreement to share the costs of constructing a new station at Caerphilly. In the event, however, neither the Barry passenger train service nor that company's financial contribution towards the cost of rebuilding ever materialised. The first stage of the redevelopment involved the relocation of the goods yard to the east of the junction with the Machen line, the new facility being opened in 1911. The passenger station was then rebuilt on an impressive scale. By the time of the final Board of Trade inspection report, dated 25th November, 1914, four through platform faces had been provided, with a new station building, alongside the road bridge, spanning the four running lines. Two pairs of double lines had been provided between Caerphilly West and East Junctions, although the Machen line could only be reached from the northern pair. Under the new arrangements, Newport trains crossed over to the northern (relief) lines at Caerphilly West Junction, while Rhymney main line trains generally used those to the south.

An '84XX' 0-6-0PT departs for Machen from Caerphilly on 14th September, 1956. Caerphilly East signal box is in the centre of this view, while the Cardiff and Caerphilly line runs straight ahead. *D. K. Jones*

Little then changed at Caerphilly until the 1960s. Caerphilly East signal box was closed on 20th July, 1964, in conjunction with the extensive rationalisation of the station layout. As a result of these changes the former down relief line became the up and down Machen single line, the old up relief being retained as a down goods loop through the station. This arrangement proved quite short-lived, however, the Machen line closing on 20th November, 1967 and the goods loop being taken out of use on 29th September, 1968. A bus station was subsequently built on the site of the former Newport platforms.

Caerphilly-Newport

From Caerphilly East Junction the first 37 chains of the line to Machen were Rhymney Railway property, the railway curving past Caerphilly goods yard to an end-on junction with the Caerphilly branch of the B&MR. A ticket platform had existed on the branch just beyond the junction. Caerphilly goods yard, by then used for domestic coal traffic only, was closed on 28th October, 1983.

The line then continued in a north-easterly direction, past the site of the junction with a siding to Rhos Llantwit Colliery (which ceased production on 30th September, 1892), to Gwernydomen (7 m. 29 ch.), the

Gwernydomen Halt on the former B&MR Caerphilly branch on 4th October, 1957, much as it was before closure. *D. K. Jones*

A Pontypridd-Machen auto-train arrives at Fountain Bridge Halt on the former Machen Loop Line.
R. W. A. Jones

Waterloo Halt looking remarkably pristine. The local press had great fun making comparisons between this diminutive stopping place and its somewhat more impressive namesake.
R. W. A. Jones

first of the Brecon & Merthyr Railway-built halts between Caerphilly and Machen. Originally a timber-built structure, from 1929 this consisted of little more than a short ground level platform, a nameboard and a lamp on each side of the line.

At Gwaun-y-Bara (7 m. 13 ch.) the down line (the Machen Loop Line, constructed by the PC&NR) parted company with the up (the earlier Caerphilly branch of the B&MR). A junction had been laid in the single line at this point in 1888 to facilitate the construction of the Machen Loop Line. This continued in use after the opening for goods and mineral traffic in November 1890 until the introduction of normal double line working between Caerphilly and Machen in September 1891, after which it was removed.

On 5th July, 1899 the Brecon & Merthyr Railway board agreed to the removal of the crossover and signalling from the junction with Rhos Llantwit Colliery Siding to Gwaun-y-Bara. This crossover was installed at the site of the earlier junction at the latter place, together with sidings off the up and down lines, the whole being reported to be complete and ready for inspection on 11th January, 1901. An additional crossover, about 300 yards to the east of the original one, was provided in 1912. This was taken out of use on 1st December, 1946. Gwaun-y-Bara signal box, which formed an intermediate block post between Caerphilly East Junction and Machen, was closed on 25th March, 1956, when the remaining crossover and sidings were also taken out of use.

Beyond Gwaun-y-Bara the up line followed the south side of the valley, before bridging the River Rhymney and climbing at 1 in 39 towards Machen station (5 m. 1 ch.). After running alongside this line for about ¼ mile, the PC&NR-built down line curved away to the north-east, across the valley and the river, to run parallel to the B&MR main line for the last mile into Machen, the ruling gradient being a relatively modest 1 in 200. Fountain Bridge halt (6 m. 32 ch.) was situated on the down (ex-PC&NR) line, with Waterloo (6 m. 18 ch.) on the up (B&MR) line.

Approaching Machen, the B&MR-built up line rapidly gained height relative to the Machen Loop Line until the two ran as a normal double track railway into the junction with the Brecon & Merthyr Railway main line. The main line itself had been single line to the west of this junction until a second line of rails was opened between Maesycwmmer and Machen on 14th December, 1896.

Machen was a typical B&MR passing station which gained greater importance as an interchange for the Pontypridd service following the drastic timetable alterations of January 1917. It consisted of up and down platforms with a rendered two-storey station building on the up

A Pontypridd-Machen auto-train gets a clear road on the former Machen Loop Line to the west of Machen on 29th August, 1956. The former B&MR main line, which ran parallel with the loop line to Machen, is visible in the extreme right of this view.

D. K. Jones

The three lines come together to the west of Machen: the single line to the left is the former Caerphilly branch of the B&MR (up line); the former Machen Loop Line (built by the PC&NR) with a line of wagons in the adjacent siding; and the double track ex-B&MR main line on the right, 14th September, 1956.

D. K. Jones

Machen station in pre-First World War days. At this time GWR trains between Pontypridd and Newport called here. *Author's collection*

side and a stone-built waiting shelter on the down. A centrally-placed trailing crossover enabled terminating trains to set back from the down to the up line before returning to Pontypridd. The goods yard, situated to the rear of the up platform, was closed on 16th July, 1964, the sidings being taken out of use on 9th August.

At the east end of Machen station the B&MR line passed beneath a stone arched bridge, turning sharply to the right, the radius being tight enough to warrant check rails. It had then passed through the company's locomotive works, until diverted to the south of the shops over a distance of 17 chains on 10th May, 1908. Machen Shops were closed from 19th March, 1927. A down relief line between Machen and Machen Shops had been brought into use on 3rd February, 1896.

Beyond Machen, trains called at Church Road (3 m. 58 ch. and downgraded to halt status on 15th September, 1952, before closing on 16th September, 1957) and Rhiwderin (3 m. 38 ch.) stations (closed to passengers on 1st March, 1954, and to goods on 14th September, 1959), before arriving at Bassaleg (0 m. 23 ch.). Church Road station signal box had become an intermediate block post on 13th November, 1905.

The approach to Bassaleg station was past extensive sidings, with the main B&MR locomotive depot on the down side of the line. The original shed, opened in 1875, was replaced by a new larger facility, closer to the

Trailer No. 103 is propelled over the crossover from the down to the up line at Machen, 13th September, 1951. The position of the crossover meant that the train would then have to set back into the up platform before forming the 7.25 pm to Pontypridd.

H. C. Casserley

Church Road station, the first stop along the B&MR line from Machen, looking towards Newport in pre-Grouping days. *Author's collection*

passenger station, in 1921. This was closed on 31st March, 1929, but the building itself was later re-erected at Kidderminster. Bassaleg North signal box was destroyed by fire on 4th July, 1909, its replacement being brought into use on 1st August of that year. This box was eventually closed on 30th May, 1965.

Bassaleg station was sandwiched between the eastern end of the sidings and Bassaleg Viaduct, originally built by the Old Rumney and bearing a plaque 'Rumney Railway Co. 1826'. The station (latterly 'South') signal box stood on the western extremity of the up platform and was closed on 10th May, 1966.

Beyond the viaduct the B&MR main line curved to the south to join the Western Valleys Line of the GWR at Bassaleg Junction. The junction signal box had opened in 1899 in conjunction with the quadrupling of the section from Bassaleg northwards to Pontymister. It was closed over the weekend of 7th-9th December, 1968 when the connections between the former B&MR lines and the Western Valleys Line were taken out, leaving the two routes as independent lines running parallel to Park Junction. The Western Valleys Line was singled in November 1981.

From Bassaleg Junction the Pontypridd-Caerphilly-Newport passenger trains ran over the Western Valleys Line (including the Tredegar Park Mile) to Park Junction, then via the spur (opened in 1879)

A well-known view of Bassaleg (B&MR) station in pre-Grouping days, but the most significant feature from our point of view is that it shows a GWR train working between Newport and Pontypridd entering the station. *L&GRP*

The limited-stop train to Pontypridd at Newport on the last day of service, 15th September, 1956, hauled by '57XX' 0-6-0PT No. 3714. *D. K. Jones*

to Gaer Junction and the South Wales main line. They then passed through Newport Tunnel into High Street station. Prior to 1912 this station had only two through platforms, with an up bay at the east end, and a down bay at the west. Trains from the PC&NR, B&MR, and Sirhowy and Western Valleys Lines arrived at the up main platform, and departed from the down bay. The up bay was converted into a through line in 1912 and was subsequently lengthened as part of the enlargement works of 1926-28, so as to enable the whole of this traffic to be dealt with on the north side of the station. New station buildings on the down side of the station were completed in 1930.

Bassaleg-Alexandra Docks

The Bassaleg-Alexandra Docks line of the PC&NR (known as the Alexandra Dock Line by the GWR) had originally left the Brecon & Merthyr Railway immediately beyond the viaduct over the River Ebbw, to the east of Bassaleg station. As opened in 1886, the junction (0 m. 18 ch.) itself was of a type then rare, but now commonplace, involving a facing crossover and a single lead connection to the PC&NR line. The latter became double at Bassaleg Loop signal box, to the south of this junction, while the B&MR line joined the Western Valleys Line of the Great Western Railway at Bassaleg Junction.

Bassaleg Loop signal box was closed on 16th August, 1925 with the provision of a new double junction between the ex-B&MR line and the Alexandra Dock Line, some 11 chains nearer to Bassaleg Junction. The dock lines at this place were converted into sidings on 20th October, 1963, accessed by a trailing connection off the former B&MR up line. This was taken out of use on 1st December, 1968.

At the Grouping in 1922 the Bassaleg-Alexandra Docks line was made up of the following sections:

- Bassaleg-northern end of the Tredegar Park Mile Railway (AD&R) 18 chains
- TPMR (owned by Lord Tredegar and used by the AD&R) 1mile 5 chains
- Southern end of TPMR-East Mendalgief Junction (AD&R) 1 mile 0 chains

The total length of line between the junction with the B&MR and East Mendalgief Junction was 2 miles 23 chains. The central section had started life as part of a tramroad from the Sirhowy Valley to Newport, authorised in 1802 and opened three years later. Converted into a standard gauge railway by 1855, the original Tredegar Park Mile Railway was used by the PC&NR from 1885. In 1922 it formed the southernmost pair of the three sets of double lines through Tredegar Park, alongside the relief lines (1885) and main lines (1898) used by the GWR.

The Alexandra Dock Line continued parallel with the Western Valleys Line to just beyond Park Junction. It then curved away to the south, crossing the Western Loop (Park Junction-Ebbw Junction) and the South Wales main line, to West Mendalgief signal box, at the west end of Mendalgief Sidings. A replacement box was opened by the GWR on 3rd February, 1928 and closed on 20th May, 1960. The up storage sidings here were removed by 1961, with the down following in 1967. The former PC&NR line joined the docks lines of the AD&R at East Mendalgief Junction. The signal box here lasted until 1976.

Alexandra Docks Engine Sheds

As this study is primarily concerned with the history of the railways built by the PC&NR Co., a survey of the dock lines of the AD&R will not be attempted. However, given their importance to the operation of the line, it will be appropriate to include reference to the engine sheds that were served off these lines. The first shed was on the south side of the original Alexandra (later North) Dock. An opening date of 1875 has been suggested elsewhere, but an Alexandra Dock Co. Minute of 22nd July, 1879 states that '...a locomotive shed was being proceeded with'. With the opening of the South Dock in 1893 access to this shed became dependent upon a swing bridge over the connecting channel between the two docks.

By 1896 the original shed had become inadequate for the needs of the growing traffic, and on 21st July a recommendation that a new building be erected near the gas works at Pill was accepted and referred to the Alexandra Docks & Railway engineer for implementation. The new shed was ready for use on 15th May, 1897. It was 240 feet long, built of brick with a northlight roof, and was situated just beyond East Mendalgief Junction. It was extended by the Great Western Railway in 1929, when a new coaling stage was also provided. Newport Pill Shed, by then '86B', closed on 17th June, 1963, the remaining allocation of twelve engines being transferred to the ex-GWR shed at Ebbw Junction. The latter shed was officially closed with effect from 4th October, 1965.

Locomotives outside the AD&R locomotive shed at East Mendalgief Junction.

Author's collection

Chapter Eight

Locomotive and Train Working

Goods and Minerals 1884-1906

The promoters of the Pontypridd, Caerphilly & Newport Railway made no provision at all for locomotive power, it being assumed, from the outset, that the traffic over their line would be worked by another company. They looked first to the B&MR to perform this function, and on 9th August, 1877 that company's directors indicated that they would be prepared to provide the necessary engines and work the traffic of the new line. Powers to enter into working agreements with both the Brecon & Merthyr and the Taff Vale Railways were included in the PC&NR Act of August 1878, although just how the impoverished B&MR was to fulfil this role remains unclear. However, this question soon became of academic interest only with the conclusion of the agreement of June 1884, under which the TVR was to supply locomotive power and work the PC&NR mineral traffic between Pontypridd and Bassaleg.

On 3rd July, 1884 the B&MR issued its first working timetable for PC&NR loaded and empty mineral trains passing between Caerphilly and Bassaleg. This gave three workings each way, with down trains departing Caerphilly at 11.30 am, 2.55 pm and 5.30 pm, and up trains leaving Bassaleg at 12.25 pm, 3.30 pm and 6.45 pm. By the following September, however, up to eight loaded trains a day were being worked over this section. Initially, trains were hauled direct from Pontypridd to Bassaleg, for exchange with the GWR, with B&MR engines banking up the Machen incline. Not without reason did TVR drivers refer to the line as 'Hell or Machen'. These trains were subject to the minimum of shunting en route, in marked contrast to contemporary practice on the TVR main line where nearly all down loaded trains (often over 70 wagons) shunted at intermediate colliery sidings, resulting in protracted delays and a generally wasteful use of locomotive power.

With the introduction of through working to Alexandra Dock in October 1887, two Taff Vale Railway engines were shedded at Newport Pill for the Pontypridd, Caerphilly & Newport Railway traffic.

The B&MR working timetable for 1897 gave no less than 18 booked paths per day for PC&NR loaded trains between Caerphilly and Bassaleg, with a similar number for returning empties. This necessitated signal boxes on this section being kept open 24 hours per day, because '...the Taff Vale Co.'s mineral trains require to run at irregular intervals'. However, it is clear that not all paths would have been taken up, but were retained to ensure maximum flexibility for TVR train working. As an illustration, PC&NR mineral traffic in 1893 (446,375 tons) would have required an average of only about six loaded trains per day.

At the opening of the PC&NR in 1884 goods and mineral traffic on the TVR was almost entirely in the hands of 0-6-0 tender engines, with the first 0-6-2T engine not appearing until the following year. A census of loaded and empty mineral trains passing between Rhondda Cutting Junction and PC&NR Junction (some running to or from the PC&NR) taken on 18th November, 1889 reveals that of a total of 39 engines recorded, nine were early (1864-1872) standard type 0-6-0s, 29 were later (1874-1889) standard 0-6-0s, and only one was an 0-6-2T.

At first the new 0-6-2Ts (later classes 'M' and 'M1') were used mainly on Taff Vale Railway passenger duties, but they soon proved their usefulness on mineral traffic, including that over the PC&NR. On 30th April, 1891 a collision occurred at Interchange Sidings, Pontypridd, involving two members of this class. A down mineral train, consisting of 29 loaded wagons hauled by brand new 0-6-2T No. 180, had stopped at Penrhos Junction to take water. On restarting, the rear portion of the train was found to have broken loose. The wagons and brake van involved then ran back to Interchange Sidings, where they collided with sister locomotive No. 148. This engine, which was working bunker first, was being driven by David Williams. His son, David Thomas Williams,

An early view of Caerphilly station showing the goods yard on the north side of the line.
C. W. Harris collection

who was acting as fireman, was badly scalded in the accident and died shortly afterwards.

The 'M' class 0-6-2Ts were the first of several broadly similar classes introduced by the TVR. Full details can be found in Part 10 of *The Locomotives of the Great Western Railway* published by the Railway Correspondence & Travel Society, but the mixed traffic engines built before 1906 may be summarised as follows:

Class	Number built	Built by	To stock
M/M1	41	Kitson & Co.; TVR	1885-1892
N	10	Kitson & Co.	1891
O	6	TVR	1894-1895
O1	14	Kitson & Co.; TVR	1894/1897
O2	9	Neilson, Reid & Co.	1899
O3	15	Hudswell, Clarke & Co.; Kitson & Co.; Vulcan Foundry	1902-1905

From 1894 the Locomotive Committee Minutes of the TVR provide some details of incidents involving the company's engines working between Pontypridd and Newport:

Date	Incident	Loco No.	Class	Type	Location
8.12.1894	Failure	144	M	0-6-2T	Caerphilly
4.5.1895	Failure	148	M	0-6-2T	Caerphilly
22.6.1895	Failure	179	M	0-6-2T	Machen
1.7.1899	Failure	7	K	0-6-0	Between Pontypridd and Newport
3.11.1899	Derailed	139	K	0-6-0	Interchange Sidings
8.12.1899	Collision	38	K	0-6-0	Penrhos (with RhyR No. 50)
26.11.1900	Derailed	52	K	0-6-0	Mendalgief
5.10.1900	Derailed	183	N	0-6-2T	Between Bassaleg and Mendalgief
9.3.1904	Collision	14	M	0-6-2T	Bassaleg Loop (with AD&R No. 5)

Whilst not a complete record by any means, this information suggests that the standard 0-6-0s and earlier 0-6-2Ts continued to provide the mainstay of locomotive power for mineral traffic between Pontypridd and Newport, although later types may well have appeared in the last years of Taff Vale Railway working.

AD&R engines also appeared on goods and mineral traffic over the PC&NR lines during the period between 1884 and 1906. From 19th March, 1886 to 18th October, 1887 they handled all loaded and empty mineral trains passing over the independent line between Bassaleg, where exchange with TVR engines took place, and Alexandra Dock.

From April 1888 negotiations took place for the B&MR's traffic to Alexandra Dock to be worked by AD&R engines via the PC&NR route

Alexandra Docks Railway locomotive No. 15.   *Author's collection*

from Bassaleg. On 20th November, 1888 the B&MR general manager reported that 'in future' all of the Powell Duffryn Co.'s traffic off the company's line, destined for the dock, would be worked this way. However, B&MR coal via this route does not appear in the PC&NR traffic returns until 1890, when just over 22,000 tons were recorded. Relatively little coal traffic was worked this way until 1893, when the total handled surged to 242,396 tons. AD&R engines also worked modest amounts of other traffic over this section throughout the PC&NR period.

AD&R engines were also used in place of those of the B&MR to bank mineral trains up Machen incline prior to the opening of the Machen Loop Line, the first recorded instance being on 15th December, 1884. The need for banking engines between Caerphilly and Machen ceased with the opening of the loop line in 1890.

On 20th April, 1891 Alexandra Docks & Railway engines started working stone traffic from Glyntaff Quarry through to Newport, but this must have been short-lived, as nothing was recorded in 1892.

It also appears that AD&R engines sometimes worked through to Interchange Sidings, Pontypridd, without B&MR authority. On 25th April, 1902 the B&MR board heard from their traffic manager that the AD&R had, on more than one occasion and 'contrary to usage', worked empty coal wagons back from Alexandra Docks to Pontypridd in this manner, and that an objection had been lodged against this practice.

Once again readers are referred to Part 10 of *The Locomotives of the Great Western Railway* for full details, but the following table lists the engines of the AD&R for the period between 1884 and 1906:

No.	Name	Type	Origin	Builder	Built	To AD&R	Withdrawn
1	Sir G. Elliot	0-6-0T	LNWR	R. Stephenson & Co.	1848	1875	1898
2	Lord Tredegar	0-6-0T	LNWR	R. Stephenson & Co.	1848	1875	1898
3	J. R. Maclean	0-6-0T	LNWR	R. & W. Hawthorn	1848	1876	1900
4	Rhondda	0-6-0T	LNWR	R. & W. Hawthorn	1849	1877	1900
5	J. C. Parkinson	0-6-0T	LNWR	Worcester Eng. Co.	1868	1879	1926
6	Lady Tredegar	0-6-0T	LNWR	Sharp	1848	1880	1906
7	Pontypridd	0-6-2T	LNWR	Sharp	1857	1880	1900
8	Aberdare Valley	0-6-0T	new	Stephenson & Co.	1880	1880	1906
9	Pontypridd	0-6-0T	LBSCR	Brighton	1866	1882	1904
10	Caerphilly	0-6-0T	LBSCR	Brighton	1866	1882	1904
11	Alexandria	0-6-0T	new	Beyer, Peacock & Co.	1871	1883	1900
12		0-6-0T	new	R. & W. Hawthorn & Co.	1884	1884	1930
13		0-6-0T	new	R. & W. Hawthorn & Co.	1884	1884	1926
14		0-6-0T	LBSCR	Brighton	1868	1885	1906
15		0-6-0T	new	R. Stephenson & Co.	1885	1885	1929
16		0-6-0T	new	Hawthorn Leslie & Co.	1885	1889	1937
17		0-6-0T	new	Hawthorn Leslie & Co.	1885	1889	1924
18		0-6-0T	new	Peckett	1890	1890	1929
19		0-6-0T	new	Peckett	1886	1890	1948
20		0-6-0T	new	R. Stephenson & Co.	1894	1894	1925
21		0-6-0T	new	R. Stephenson & Co.	1894	1894	1926
Replacement stock							
1		0-6-0T	new	R. Stephenson & Co.	1898	1898	1929
2		0-6-0T	new	R. Stephenson & Co.	1898	1898	1926
3		0-6-0T	new	R. Stephenson & Co.	1900	1900	1929
4		0-6-0T	new	R. Stephenson & Co.	1900	1900	1929
5		0-6-0T	new	R. Stephenson & Co.	1900	1900	1925

In addition, the Alexandra Docks & Railway possessed various 0-4-0ST engines which were used for shunting around the docks sidings.

Two accidents of note involving Taff Vale Railway-worked mineral trains took place in the period running up to the takeover of such workings by the AD&R. On 20th December, 1904 one of these trains came to grief on the Caerphilly branch. Owing to a breakage of coupling links 67 wagons ran back on the down line and went off the road at catch points at Gwaun-y-Bara signal box. Considerable damage was done to the permanent way, both lines being blocked for over 8 hours. A similar mishap occurred on 29th July, 1905 when 59 wagons broke loose at Bassaleg and ran back, colliding with wagons standing in a siding. Six Brecon & Merthyr Railway trucks were totally destroyed.

Pontypridd-Caerphilly-Newport Passenger Service

The decision to operate a passenger service between Pontypridd, Caerphilly and Newport brought with it a requirement for a suitable engine and a set of coaches. The former was provided by the AD&R, with 0-6-0T No. 10 *Caerphilly* being the usual motive power, although sister engine No. 9 *Pontypridd* may also have been used. Both had been built at Brighton in August 1866 for the London, Brighton & South Coast Railway to a design by J. C. Craven, and had been acquired by the AD&R in 1882, subsequently being fitted with cabs and larger bunkers.

The PC&NR Co.'s first thoughts concerning passenger coaches were directed towards second-hand vehicles. On 27th September, 1887 Edmund Creed, the company's secretary, was instructed to see Mr Scotter, general manager of the LSWR, to see if that company would be prepared to sell or lend any surplus carriages. He was also to ascertain the prices of new stock from the Metropolitan Carriage & Wagon Co. of Birmingham.

Mr Scotter offered various specimens, but Mr Creed was not impressed, stating that they 'would have compared unfavourably with the carriages of the Great Western, Taff Vale and Brecon & Merthyr Railways'. Creed then approached the B&MR, which was awaiting delivery of a new set of carriages from the Metropolitan C. & W. Co. On 19th October, 1887 that company's traffic & works committee agreed to an extension of the delivery period for the new coaches to 1st April,

Carriage No. 2 of the PC&NR. *Author's collection*

1888. The effect of this decision was to allow the PC&NR to acquire the four vehicles being built by the Metropolitan C. & W. Co., with a further set then being constructed for later delivery to the B&MR.

The four coaches, which were delivered in time for the start of the passenger service in December 1887 at total cost of £1,165 17s., were all four-wheeled and comprised:

No. 1:	Four compartment brake/third;
No. 2:	Five compartment third;
No. 3:	Four compartment first/second composite; and
No. 4:	Single compartment third/luggage/brake.

The inaugural service was somewhat limited, consisting of only three trains each way, Mondays to Saturdays:

Pontypridd	dep.	8.35 am	11.20 am	4.50 pm
Caerphilly	arr.	8.55	11.35	5.08
Newport	arr.	9.25	12.0 pm	5.35
Newport	dep.	9.50 am	2.55 pm	7.05 pm
Caerphilly	dep.	11.20	3.25	7.43
Pontypridd	arr.	10.35	3.50	8.00

The trains also called at Machen, Church Road, Rhiwderin and Bassaleg. The locomotive and coaches used were originally based at Glyntaff, but this proved a short-lived arrangement. On 14th July, 1891 the PC&NR board heard that it was intended to improve the service with effect from 1st August. This involved an additional train each way, with the stock being transferred from Glyntaff to Alexandra Dock. It also required a modification to the agreement with the GWR for the use of High Street station, Newport, together with the payment of additional tolls and rent. The revised timetable gave:

Pontypridd	dep.	8.35 am	11.20 am	4.50 pm	8.15 pm
Caerphilly	arr.	8.53	11.35	5.08	8.33
Newport	arr.	9.25	12.02 pm	5.15	9.05
Newport	dep.	7.30 am	9.50 am	2.50 pm	7.05 pm
Caerphilly	dep.	8.02	10.20	3.25	7.43
Pontypridd	arr.	8.20	10.35	3.50	8.00

With the Pontypridd, Caerphilly & Newport Railway possessing only one set of coaches, it was necessary for the company to borrow or hire replacement vehicles whenever its own were not available for service. On 30th September, 1891 the B&MR agreed to loan a train to the PC&NR so that its coaches could be fitted with vacuum brakes.

By the Autumn of 1894 the PC&NR train was becoming rather decrepit, and on 6th November Alfred Henshaw, the company's general manager, advised that if the service was to be continued then '...some provision for having the train done up must be made.' This work was carried out by the Gloucester Carriage & Wagon Co., which also undertook to provide a replacement set of coaches for use by the PC&NR. Nevertheless, on 14th January, 1895 the B&MR 'loaned' three of its coaches to the company at a charge, as on previous occasions, of 10s. per day. However, in spite of this fairly extensive refurbishment, the PC&NR coaches needed new doors in 1897, these being fitted by the Metropolitan Carriage & Wagon Co.

The PC&NR train was involved in a number of accidents over the years. On 20th August, 1896, as the train was approaching Church Road station on the B&MR, the leading axle of locomotive No. 10 broke, causing a wheel to leave the rails. Little damage resulted and the train was stopped without injury. The engine and first passenger coach were derailed on 15th September, 1897, when the 9.40 am train from Newport was approaching Pontypridd station, while the breakage of a locomotive axle near Bassaleg was reported on 17th December of that year.

With the opening of the Rhondda & Swansea Bay Railway through to Swansea in 1895, local dissatisfaction with the GWR service between that town and Newport led to demands for the development of a somewhat unlikely competitive route, via the R&SBR, TVR, and PC&NR. Both the R&SBR and the TVR were very keen to see this introduced, but the PC&NR was much more cautious, no doubt fearing the wrath of the GWR. On 17th December, 1897 the PC&NR board rejected a request from the R&SBR for a through coach to be added to the Newport train at Pontypridd. Faced with this impasse the R&SBR and the TVR came to a separate arrangement, and in 1898 brought in through working over each others lines between Swansea and Cardiff, via Treherbert.

This development came at a time when negotiations were progressing for the takeover of the PC&NR passenger service by the GWR. The TVR was clearly not happy with this prospect, and reacted with alarm in November 1897, when GWR engines appeared at Pontypridd hauling the PC&NR train. However, normal working with an AD&R engine was resumed on 29th November.

There was a widespread expectation that the quality of the Pontypridd-Caerphilly-Newport service would improve once it had been taken over by the GWR. However, these hopes were frustrated when the GWR trains appeared on 2nd January, 1899. The timetable continued to show only four trains each way, Mondays to Saturdays,

LOCOMOTIVE AND TRAIN WORKING 141

with the ex-PC&NR coaches being replaced by GWR vehicles of similar vintage and standard. Trains were hauled by 0-6-0ST engines based at Newport (High Street) Shed. The four ex-PC&NR coaches were reported to be at Alexandra Docks on 17th January, 1899, when the AD&R board decided to retain them for the company's own use rather than sell them. Their eventual fate is not known but they appear to have gone by 1904.

Minerals Traffic under the AD&R

In February 1903 the Mersey Railway (MyR) Co. offered for sale 18 locomotives and 97 carriages, all of which had been rendered surplus as a result of the electrification of its line. With the working agreement with the TVR due to expire towards the end of 1905, the AD&R grasped this opportunity and purchased six 2-6-2T engines which had been built by Beyer Peacock & Co. in 1887. The first three (MyR Nos. 12, 13 and 15) were delivered in November 1903, at a total cost of £1,750, with the remainder (MyR Nos. 10, 11 and 14) following in May 1904 for £1,700.

On 24th January, 1905 the AD&R board authorised the purchase of more Mersey Railway locomotives at a total cost of £2,325, together with a spare set of cylinders. Of these engines three were 0-6-4Ts built by Beyer, Peacock in 1895 (MyR Nos. 2, 3, and 6) while the fourth (My R No. 16) was a 2-6-2T built by Kitson & Co. in 1892.

The ex-Mersey Railway engines (which also lost their names) were renumbered by the AD&R as follows:

MyR No.	MyR Name	AD&R No.	GW No.	Type
2	Earl of Chester	24	1346	0-6-4T
3	Duke of Lancaster	23	1345	0-6-4T
6	Fox	22	1344	0-6-4T
10	Mersey	7	1208	2-6-2T
11	Victoria	6	1207	2-6-2T
12	Bouverie	9	1211	2-6-2T
13	Brunlees	10	1201	2-6-2T
14	Tranmere	8	1209	2-6-2T
15	Salisbury	11	1204	2-6-2T
16	Burcot	25	1199	2-6-2T

The AD&R removed the redundant condensing equipment from all these engines, and also provided them with enclosed cabs by adding a roof to the front weather board. It is thought likely that their first duties would have included B&MR coal traffic from Bassaleg to Alexandra Docks, via the independent line through Tredegar Park. With its takeover of the Pontypridd-Newport mineral traffic in May 1906 the AD&R was able to employ the ex-Mersey Railway engines to good effect, hauling coal from Interchange Sidings, Pontypridd through to Mendalgief Sidings.

In addition to procuring suitable locomotive power, the AD&R was faced with other expenses as a result of taking over the working of its mineral traffic. On 24th April, 1906 its board had authorised the alteration of B&MR platform walls and other items to provide the necessary clearance for the larger ex-MyR engines. Additional brake vans were also needed, with four being ordered from the Glasgow Engineering Co. in June 1906, and another, from the same source, in the following June. On 22nd January, 1907 the AD&R board confirmed an order for a 20 ton steam breakdown crane, to be supplied by Jessop and Appleby Brothers of Leicester and London for £2,104.

An accident which could have had serious consequences for the management of the AD&R occurred on 5th October, 1906, when one of its ex-Mersey Railway 0-6-4Ts No. 24, which had been shunting at the up sidings to the west of Basseleg, collided with the locomotive and leading coach of an AD&R special train conveying John Macaulay, the general manager, and other officers of the company. Fortunately, all of these gentlemen, who were travelling in the second compartment on their way to inspect the new works at Pontypridd, escaped injury.

The accident on 5th October, 1906 at Basseleg *J. Dore Dennis collection*

Later that month an AD&R empty mineral train was derailed on the up line of the Caerphilly branch. Twenty-two wagons were badly damaged, five being completely destroyed.

A significant development concerning mineral traffic working occurred on 1st July, 1913 when B&MR loaded and empty coal trains started running through to and from Mendalgief Sidings via the former PC&NR route, without change of engine at Bassaleg.

Pontypridd-Caerphilly: Motor Cars and Trains

The AD&R ordered its first Motor Car from the Glasgow Railway & Engineering Co. of Govan in February 1904 for use between Pontypridd (Tram Road) and Caerphilly. Dugald Drummond, designer of the inspirational LSWR/LBSCR cars, had a financial interest in the Glasgow Railway & Engineering Co. and acted as consulting engineer to the AD&R in the design of its Car No. 1. This vehicle followed the general principles of Drummond's cars, but with the locomotive unit completely enclosed within the body of the coach. The car was 56 ft 6 in. long, with a low arc roof, the locomotive unit having a vertical boiler and two 9 in. x 14 in. cylinders acting on the front wheels. Seating was provided for 52 passengers, all third class.

The Motor Car service, which commenced on 1st September, 1904, comprised seven round trips between Pontypridd (Tram Road) and Caerphilly, these being additional to the four GWR trains each way between Pontypridd, Caerphilly and Newport.

To provide back up for Car No. 1 the AD&R purchased three four-wheeled coaches from the Mersey Railway in September 1904 for £150. An order for an additional second-hand coach, this time from the Glyncorrwg Colliery Co., was confirmed on 22nd October, 1907.

To improve the frequency of the Pontypridd-Caerphilly service an additional car was required. The purchase of Car No. 2 was authorised on 23rd May, 1905, the order once again being placed with the Glasgow Railway & Engineering Co. The new car, which arrived at Newport on 16th September, was larger than Car No. 1, being an inch short of 65 feet in length. It had a clerestory roof, curving down at the ends in the American fashion, and could seat 54 passengers. In both cars steam regulation, reversing gear and brakes were arranged to be worked from either end of the car by means of rods and levers. Communication between the fireman and the driver (when at the opposite end) was by means of a speaking tube and electric bells.

The introduction of Car No. 2 enabled a more frequent service to be introduced on 1st May, 1906, with twelve Pontypridd-Caerphilly and thirteen return trips. This pattern, which involved an empty car working to Caerphilly in the early morning, lasted until 1910, when the first Caerphilly-Pontypridd car was withdrawn, leaving a balanced twelve trips each way. The timetable then stayed in this form until its curtailment during the First World War. On 4th June, 1911 a Sunday service was trialed, the notice announcing this innovation warning that:

> The Sunday service will be provisional and experimental and the Company do not bind themselves to the continuance thereof.

This somewhat cautionary tone proved to be justified: the experiment was not a success, and the service did not appear in the summer timetable for 1912.

The Rhymney Railway Motor Car service between Caerphilly and Machen, introduced on 1st April, 1908, consisted of five round trips, running in addition to the four through Great Western Railway trains each way over this section. The timetable remained in this form through to 1910, but by the following summer it was down to only three Caerphilly-Machen return trips daily.

Two mixed traffic '1661' class 0-6-0STs were acquired from the Great Western Railway in November 1906. Nos. 1679 and 1683, which had previously been on hire to the AD&R at a rental of 5s. per hour each 'when in steam', were given the numbers 27 and 28 by their new owners. No. 28 and a brake van were derailed in spectacular fashion at Bassaleg on 4th January, 1907. Having accepted the AD&R engine and van off the former PC&NR line, the signalman in the Brecon & Merthyr Railway signal box at the junction then decided to give precedence to an up passenger train. Accordingly, he reversed the points on the AD&R line returned the signal to 'danger' and accepted the up passenger. The AD&R engine, which had started moving when its signal was lowered, was unable to stop in time and ran through the trap points before it rolled down the embankment, which at this point was about 30 feet high. Fortunately, the crew were able to jump clear and were uninjured, while the guard was only slightly hurt. The B&MR signalman was found to be at fault, no blame being attributed to the AD&R driver.

The popularity of the Motor Car service between Pontypridd and Caerphilly soon gave rise to problems of overcrowding. Failures could also prove very disruptive. Fortunately, the AD&R was able, once again, to take advantage of the second-hand market to satisfy its requirements.

On 27th October, 1908 its board confirmed the expenditure of £450 on the purchase of three passenger coaches from E. E. Cornforth of Trentham, Staffordshire. These were of a highly distinctive appearance (to British eyes, at least), having been built by W. R. Renshaw of Stoke-on-Trent in 1898 for use in Barnum & Bailey's 'Greatest Show on Earth' touring train, and were bogie saloon vehicles of the American type with open verandas at each end and clerestory roofs. However, having obtained the coaches at bargain price, the AD&R was then faced with a substantially greater expense in adapting them for use on its railway. On 23rd March, 1909 the board approved the expenditure of £495 11s on converting two of these coaches for use between Pontypridd and Caerphilly. Conversion of the third coach was authorised on 27th July, at a cost of £370. As altered the Barnum & Bailey coaches were used as trailers for the Motor Cars, or formed into a train, hauled by one of the ex-GWR class '1661' 0-6-0STs, purchased in 1906.

Other ex-Barnum & Bailey vehicles were also acquired from E. E. Cornforth. On 25th October, 1910 the AD&R board authorised the conversion of a fourth coach – although not, it would appear, for passenger use – and the alteration of two elephant cars for use as portable warehouse and transit cars. Reconstruction of 18 bogie flat cars from the same source was approved on 20th December, followed by two more on 28th March, 1911.

Locomotive No. 14 purchased from the GWR in 1911, the coach nearest the engine was formerly Motor Car No. 2 and at the far end of the train is one of the Barnum and Bailey coaches. *Author's collection*

By 1911 the Motor Cars were showing distinct signs of wear and tear. It was decided, therefore, to convert Car No. 2 into a trailer, and to acquire a suitable locomotive to work with it. In February of that year the Alexandra Docks & Railway purchased an 0-4-2T engine from the Great Western Railway for this purpose. No. 1426 was a member of the '517' class, having been built at Wolverhampton in 1877, and became No. 14 under the AD&R. Car No. 2 was converted into a trailer by replacing the locomotive unit with an ordinary bogie. In this form it was renumbered No. 4 and coupled with one of the Barnum & Bailey coaches, the set then usually being worked by engine No. 14.

Car No. 1 was converted in a similar manner in 1917, becoming coach No. 5, and paired with another of the Barnum & Bailey coaches. The two sets proved sufficient for the traffic, leaving the third Barnum & Bailey coach as spare. About 1920 Barnum & Bailey coach No. 1 was taken out of normal stock and parked in a siding at Newport Pill for use as an office by the shed foreman and his clerical staff.

Two other vacuum-fitted locomotives were added to stock in 1912 and 1913, both being of GWR origin and purchased from the Bute Works Supply Co. No. 32 (GWR No. 1356 *Will Scarlet*), acquired in November 1912, had been built by Fletcher Jennings & Co. in 1873 for the Severn & Wye Railway, while No. 33 (GWR No. 993), added to stock in January 1913, was an 0-6-0ST of the '850' class.

With these acquisitions the AD&R possessed a total of five vacuum-fitted engines available for passenger train work, as follows:

AD&R No.	Former GWR No.	Description
14	1426	0-4-2T
27	1679	0-6-0ST
28	1683	0-6-0ST
32	1356	0-6-0T
33	993	0-6-0ST

Of these engines Nos. 14 and 32 appear to have been those most commonly used on such work.

The Barnum & Bailey coaches and former Motor Cars were all described as 'trailers' by the Alexandra Docks & Railway, from which it might be inferred that the two coach sets were operated as auto-trains, making use of the latter's driving ends when being propelled. However, surviving photographs show no trace of auto-gear on any of the vacuum-fitted engines, while views of the trains in action show them being hauled from either end. None of these vehicles were subsequently listed as 'trailers' by the Great Western Railway.

On Friday 4th January, 1907 locomotive No. 28 was steaming through Basseleg on its way to Pontypridd. An error by the signal man allowed the locomotive to leave the track through the catch point and topple down the embankment. The driver and fireman were able to jump clear, but the guard was trapped in the van receiving severe abrasions. The locomotive and the van were recovered and the locomotive at least returned to service.
Author's collection

One unusual train working which occurred in 1913 was deemed sufficiently important to merit a mention at a meeting of the board of the AD&R. On Easter Monday, 24th March, the Rhymney Railway worked a special passenger train from Cardiff to Pontypridd (Tram Road), via Caerphilly, making use of that company's running powers over the former PC&NR line from Penrhos Junction.

The Great War and After

A new engine shed was opened by the GWR at Ebbw Junction, to the west of Newport, on 17th July, 1915, replacing the old one at High Street station. The new depot supplied engines for the GWR's Pontypridd-Caerphilly-Newport passenger train service, but not for long.

The war years witnessed the general curtailment of passenger train services, but the major change, as far as the AD&R was concerned, came on 1st January, 1917, with the withdrawal of the GWR trains between Pontypridd and Newport, while the Rhymney Railway service between Caerphilly and Machen, which had already been cut to two trains each way per day by 1915, was reduced to a single round trip only. The AD&R trains were reduced to nine each way, with all but two being extended to run between Caerphilly and Machen, from where Newport could be reached by means of the B&MR. At the Pontypridd end these trains continued to terminate at the Tram Road station, thereby adding to the inconvenience experienced by passengers wishing to travel between the TVR system and Newport, via Caerphilly.

The surviving Rhymney working between Caerphilly and Machen had gone by May 1917. Apart from this the pattern introduced in January 1917 continued in operation up to and after the end of the war. By August 1921 one of the AD&R trains had been cut back to Caerphilly, with the gap between there and Machen being filled by a single return working by a Rhymney auto-train, leaving Caerphilly at 10.42 am and returning from Machen 10 minutes later.

The general air of post-war restrictions and austerity was relieved on 21st August, 1920, when the GWR introduced a summer season through train between Newport and Aberystwyth, running on Mondays, Fridays and Saturdays only, via the former PC&NR, Pontypridd, Treherbert and Carmarthen. This working was, in fact, the successor to a pre-war service which the TVR had operated between Pontypridd and Aberystwyth, via the Rhondda & Swansea Bay Railway, the first train to West Wales, via that route, having run on 25th July, 1903. The GWR train ran until 27th September, 1920 and reappeared in the 1921 season, but in

The last AD&R locomotive No. 37. *Author's collection*

the 1922 summer timetable, introduced on 10th July, it ran between Treherbert and Aberystwyth only. This also applied during 1923, but for the 1924 season, commencing on 14th July, the Aberystwyth train operated from Cardiff (Parade), working via Caerphilly, the former PC&NR line and Pontypridd to Treherbert, but on Mondays and Saturdays only. This routing remained in force until the end of the summer season in September 1932, but the following year the train, which had started from Cardiff (Queen Street) since 1928, was diverted via Radyr and the Taff Vale main line, running on Saturdays only.

The Cardiff-Treherbert-Carmarthen-Aberystwyth service was withdrawn on the outbreak of the Second World War, but then reinstated for two seasons only in the post-war period, before fading away like the market it had served.

September 1920 saw the delivery of the last engines ordered by the Alexandra Docks & Railway, two 2-6-2Ts, (Nos. 36 and 37), being supplied by R. & W. Hawthorn Leslie & Co. They were fitted with Belpaire fireboxes and Ross pop valves, and were put to work hauling coal trains between Interchange Sidings, Pontypridd and Mendalgief Sidings for Alexandra Docks.

At the Grouping in 1922 the AD&R possessed the following locomotives and rolling stock:

Locomotives	38
Passenger carriages (2 ex-railcars and 2 Barnum & Bailey)	4
Barnum & Bailey coach used as departmental vehicle	1
Open wagons (mostly 2 or 3 planks)	642
Special wagons (ex-Barnum & Bailey)	20
Vans (8-10 tons)	6
Goods brake vans	9
Departmental wagons	13
Steam breakdown crane	1

Post Grouping Years

The basic pattern of the passenger timetable introduced in January 1917 persisted beyond the Grouping, although the solitary Rhymney working each way between Caerphilly and Machen had gone by July 1922. On 9th July, 1923, in a bold move aimed at restoring the pre-war links between the Taff Valley and Newport, the GWR re-introduced the Pontypridd-Caerphilly-Newport through trains, increasing their number to six each way and extending them to start from and terminate at Merthyr Tydfil.

As before these trains ran non-stop between Pontypridd and Caerphilly. The local service on this section remained at nine trains each way, but with only five of these running to and from Machen. The Merthyr-Pontypridd-Caerphilly-Newport service was evidently too lavish for the traffic on offer, as from 22nd September, 1924 it was reduced to only three round trips, a level at which it was to remain until the emergency timetable, introduced in September 1939.

At its closure in September 1922 the locomotive allocation at Glyntaff Shed consisted of 0-6-0ST No. 15 and 0-4-2T No. 14. The latter was renumbered 1426 by the GWR (thereby restoring its original number), was transferred to the former TVR shed at Coke Ovens, about a mile west of Pontypridd, where it remained until October 1927, when it was moved to (ex-TVR) Aberdare Shed. No. 1426 was withdrawn in November 1934.

The post-Grouping years were not kind to most of the locomotives inherited by the GWR from the AD&R. All the ex-MyR 0-6-4Ts had gone by 1927, with the 2-6-2Ts being withdrawn between 1929 and 1932, all having remained at Newport to the end. The Hawthorn Leslie 2-6-2Ts fared rather better, staying at Newport until the war, and ending their days as shed pilots at Hereford (GWR No. 1206 (AD&R No. 37)) in 1951 and Cardiff Canton (GWR No. 1205 (AD&R No. 36)) in 1956.

The Alexandra Docks & Railway passenger carriages too did not last long under their new owners:

AD&R No.	Type	GWR No.	Date withdrawn
1	Barnum & Bailey	–	11th August, 1923 (A)
2	Barnum & Bailey	27	25th December, 1926
3	Barnum & Bailey	64	25th December, 1926
4	ex-Motor Car	90	25th October, 1930
5	ex-Motor Car	95	1st September, 1928 (B)

A – used as an office at Newport Pill
B – altered for use by locomotive department (No. 173); withdrawn 22nd September, 1934.

During 1925 and 1926 the Great Western Railway modified nine ex-Taff Vale Railway class 'M1' 0-6-2Ts for use with its mode of auto-working. Two of these engines, Nos. 484 and 487, were at Coke Ovens Shed in January 1926 and were employed on Pontypridd-Caerphilly-Machen auto-trains. The auto-fitted 0-6-2Ts were withdrawn between 1932 and 1934, the last survivor at Coke Ovens being No. 673. By this time the shed had also become home to three auto-fitted 'Metro' class 2-4-0Ts, Nos. 3595, 3597 and 3599, which were used on the branches radiating from Pontypridd, including that to Caerphilly and Machen.

LOCOMOTIVE AND TRAIN WORKING

AD&R's second locomotive No. 1 built by R. Stephenson & Co. to replace the original in 1898.
Author's collection

No. 32 ex-GWR No. 1356. *Author's collection*

On the closure of Coke Ovens Shed on 31st December, 1933, the three 'Metros' were transferred to Abercynon, from where they continued to provide locomotive power for the Pontypridd branch line services. Their numbers declined with the arrival of class '64XX' auto-fitted 0-6-0PTs, introduced in 1934, the last Abercynon 'Metro', No. 3599, being moved to Radyr Shed by the end of 1947. Merthyr and Newport Pill engines were used on the Merthyr-Pontypridd-Newport limited-stop trains, introduced in 1923, with class '57XX' 0-6-0PTs and ex-TVR class 'A' 0-6-2Ts being recorded.

In 1924 the GWR introduced the first of 200 '56XX' class 0-6-2T locomotives intended principally for work on freight trains in South Wales, where they gradually usurped the pre-Grouping types of the same configuration. On the Pontypridd-Caerphilly-Machen section examples of this class from Abercynon, Aberdare, Coke Ovens (until the end of 1933), Ebbw Junction and Pontypool Road Sheds made their presence felt in ever increasing numbers.

By 1928 the majority of mineral trains and returning empties over the former Pontypridd, Caerphilly & Newport Railway line were being worked through between Stormstown Junction and Mendalgief Sidings, with the working timetable for that year giving five booked paths each way. Whereas in AD&R days such traffic would have been wholly the responsibility of Newport engines, the GWR years saw these turns being shared with Abercynon Shed.

One legacy of wartime operations was the continued use of the Pontypridd-Caerphilly line as an alternative to the Quakers Yard route for freight traffic between Pontypridd and Pontypool Road. In 1928 there were two such workings each way, all running via Aber Junction and Ystrad Mynach:

Up
8.40 am		Pontypridd Coke Ovens-Pontypool Road
7.50 pm	SO	Ferndale-Pontypool Road
9.50 pm	SX	Ferndale-Pontypool Road

Down
11.00 pm	SX	Pontypool Road-Ferndale
5.30 am		Little Mill Junction-Pont Shon Norton
9.00 pm	SO	Pontypool Road-Ferndale

The Depression years witnessed a mass exodus of people from the South Wales valleys in search of work in other less blighted parts of the United Kingdom, with London and Slough being popular destinations. A reflection of this development was the timetabled

Paddington-Treherbert expresses that ran on August Bank Holidays from 1933. These trains were routed away from the South Wales main line, via Machen and Caerphilly, thereby avoiding the congested area around Cardiff.

Looking ahead for a moment, the post-war years were to see increased use of the Pontypridd-Caerphilly-Newport route for relief trains, particularly at Bank Holidays, between Paddington and the valleys focusing on Pontypridd. Excursions to a great variety of English (and, for rugby internationals, Scottish) destinations also passed this way. Engines were changed at Bassaleg and sometimes Newport, with pairs of 0-6-2Ts taking charge away from the South Wales main line. Such workings continued for some years after the end of the timetabled passenger service in 1956.

With the introduction of the wartime emergency timetable on 25th September, 1939, the Merthyr-Newport passenger trains were withdrawn and the local service between Pontypridd and Machen reduced in frequency. The revised timetable contained one limited-stop train each way between Pontypridd and Newport and six all stations round trips between Pontypridd and Machen, one of which ran through to and from Newport. Whereas other lines in South Wales saw some increase from this low point, the Pontypridd-Caerphilly-Machen-Newport service remained at this level throughout the war years.

Things improved slightly in the immediate post-war period. By October 1947 an additional Pontypridd-Caerphilly train each way had been added to the timetable, together with a number of Wednesdays or Saturdays only workings. This pattern continued until the introduction of the summer timetable on 14th June, 1954, when the number of trains between Pontypridd and Caerphilly was increased to eight each way, with five of these continuing to and from Machen. This improved timetable then remained in place until the withdrawal of the Pontypridd-Caerphilly-Machen passenger trains in September 1956.

In the post-Nationalisation period the Pontypridd-Caerphilly-Machen auto-trains continued to be operated by class '64XX' 0-6-0PT engines from Abercynon Shed, with Nos. 6401, 6411, 6434 and 6438 being present at the commencement of the new regime. Also recorded on working 'JF' were Nos. 6402, 6433 and 6435. The solitary Newport-Pontypridd and return limited-stop train was worked by a Newport Pill loco, with two ex-TVR 0-6-2Ts (Nos. 425 and 426) at that shed in 1948 and an ex-GWR class '41XX' 2-6-2T No. 4130 reported as being retained for this purpose in 1955. In later years 0-6-0PTs of the '57XX' and '84XX' classes were also used on this service.

For the last day of the passenger service on Saturday, 15th September, 1956 two auto-trailers were turned out for the Pontypridd-Caerphilly-Machen trains, hauled by 0-6-0PT No. 6433 in the morning, with sister engine No. 6411 taking over for the rest of the day on the 1.25 pm from Pontypridd. A class '57XX' 0-6-0PT No. 3714, with three coaches, was used on the surviving Newport-Pontypridd and return limited-stop working, being driven by Reg Young and fired by Mr O'Shea.

A number of enthusiasts' excursions worked over the former PC&NR line in its later years. On 12th July, 1952 one such railtour, organised by the Midlands Area of the Stephenson Locomotive Society (SLS) and worked by class '64XX' 0-6-0PT No. 6423 with two ex-TVR auto-trailers, ran from Pontypridd to Penrhos Junction, where it reversed onto the former Barry line. A Gloucestershire Railway Society special on 12th May, 1956 brought a 'Dean Goods' 0-6-0, No. 2538, to the line. Another SLS tour, on 11th July, 1959, saw a three-car diesel multiple unit running between Pontypridd, Caerphilly and Machen. The final steam passenger train to work over the line was an excursion jointly organised by the Monmouthshire and West Glamorgan Railway Societies on 27th June, 1964. The six-coach train, hauled by class '56XX' 0-6-2T No. 6614 and

Gloucestershire Railway Society's South Wales Rail Tour on 12th May, 1956, passing Groeswen Halt. *Author's collection*

bearing the headboard 'The Leek', ran from Park Junction to Pontypridd, via Machen and Caerphilly, in the course of its tour of a number of doomed lines in South Wales.

Locomotives of the '56XX' class of 0-6-2Ts and the '57XX' class of 0-6-0PTs provided the mainstay for locomotive power on coal trains over the Pontypridd-Caerphilly-Newport route in the last years of steam. Class '52XX' 2-8-0T engines also appeared on these workings.

All were swept aside with the influx of large numbers of English Electric Type '3' (later class '37') 1750 HP diesel electric Co-Co locomotives in South Wales from Spring 1963 onwards. Such was the pace of this change that dieselisation of the Cardiff Valleys network was completed on 24th July, 1965 with the closure of the last steam depot at Radyr (88B).

Latterly the Type '3's worked about a dozen freight trains daily over the Pontypridd-Caerphilly section between a variety of origins and destinations. The working timetable for the Cardiff Valleys for 18th April, 1966 gives the following details of local trip working over the line:

Target No.	Stabling point	Depart	Working
H33	Abercynon	21.30 SX	Stormstown-Alexandra Dock Junction
		02.10 MX	Alexandra Dock Junction-Stormstown
H20	Aberdare	06.00 MO	Abercwmboi-Severn Tunnel Junction
		10.20 MO	Severn Tunnel Junction-Aberdare
H21	Aberdare	04.15 MX	Severn Tunnel Junction-Stormstown
H23	Aberdare	07.05 MO	Abercwmboi-Park Junction
		10.30 MO	Park Junction-Aberdare
		18.05 SX	Severn Tunnel Junction-Aberdare
		01.10 MX	Severn Tunnel Junction-Aberdare
H27	Aberdare	16.50 SX	Aberdare-Severn Tunnel Junction
		21.00 SX	Severn Tunnel Junction-Aberdare
H28	Aberdare	07.55 MO	Abercwmboi-Severn Tunnel Junction
		12.30 MO	Severn Tunnel Junction-Aberdare
H33	Abecynon	21.30 SX	Stormstown-Alexandra Dock Junction
		02.10 MX	Alexandra Dock Junction-Stormstown
H36	Merthyr	19.05 SX	Merthyr-Alexandra Dock Junction
		23.20 SX	Alexandra Dock Junction-Stormstown
J06	Godfrey Road	16.05 MWF	Tymawr Colliery-Spencer Works
J35	Severn Tunnel Junction	07.45 MO	Stormstown-Severn Tunnel Junction
J50	Pontypool Road	00.25 MX	Pontypool Road-Stormstown

SX – Except Saturday, MX – Except Monday, MO – Mondays only,
MWF – Mondays, Wednesdays, Fridays

In addition, the following trips, also covered by the Type '3's, were shown working over the Caerphilly-Machen section in the same timetable:

Target No.	Stabling point	Depart	Working
H12	Radyr	06.25 MX	Aber Junction-Severn Tunnel Junction
H40	Rhymney	10.15 Daily	Bargoed-East Usk Junction
		17.35 SX	Ystrad Mynach-East Usk Junction
		21.35 SX	Bassaleg Junction-Ystrad Mynach
		14.10 SO	Machen-Bargoed
J31	Aberbeeg	04.00 MX	Nelson & Llancaiach-East Usk Junction
		20.25 SX	Ocean and Taff Merthyr-Rogerstone
J36	Severn Tunnel Junction	17.55 SX	Nelson & Llancaiach-Severn Tunnel Jct
		01.25 MX	Nelson & Llancaiach-Severn Tunnel Jct
		02.40 MX	Aber Junction-Severn Tunnel Junction

The remaining traffic was diverted via Radyr and Penarth North Curve on the closure of the two sections concerned in January and November 1967 respectively.

A 350 HP 0-6-0 diesel mechanical shunter (later class '08'), which was employed as yard pilot at Pontypridd, continued to service Glyntaff goods yard, until this remnant followed the rest of the former PC&NR lines into oblivion in July 1967.

A three coach dmu sets back over the crossover at Machen on 11th July, 1959 on an SLS excursion having just worked through from Penrhiwfelin on the Rhymney Railway via Caerphilly and Fountain Bridge to Machen. The trains then departed for Pontypridd via Waterloo Halt and the PC&NR lines. *S. Rickard collection*

Chapter Nine

Postscript

Despite the scale of the closures that have taken place over the years almost all of the pre-Grouping companies of South Wales have managed to retain a presence, however small, in the contemporary railway scene of the area. Thus the docks and certain connecting lines of the AD&R Co. still remain in productive use. Of the former PC&NR lines, however, not a trace now remains as far as operational railways are concerned.

After closure and track removal a short section of the Pontypridd-Penrhos Junction line between Glyntaff and the western end of Interchange Sidings, adjacent to the Brown, Lenox works at Pontypridd, was completely obliterated as a result of the construction of the dual carriageway A470 trunk road, opened in June 1973. The viaduct over the River Taff was dismantled during the road construction, and nearly 30 years after final closure this part of the PC&NR was used as the route for a new link road between the A470 and Pontypridd town centre.

South of Glyntaff the trackbed remained relatively undisturbed, although increasingly overgrown. Its potential for recreational use was soon recognised, however, and in 1989 Taff Ely Borough Council completed a cycleway along the section between Nantgarw and

The former PC&NR main line transformed as the 'Taff Trail'. *W.John*

Glyntaff. June 1993 saw the official launch, at Cyfarthfa Castle in Merthyr, of the 'Taff Trail' between Cardiff and Brecon, incorporating the cycleway on the route of the PC&NR. The Taff Trail subsequently came to form part of Los Las Cymru – Route No. 8 of the National Cycle Network – between Cardiff and Holyhead.

Since local government reorganisation in South Wales in 1996 the section of the Taff Trail between Nantgarw and Glyntaff has been managed by Rhondda Cynon Taff County Borough Council. The Council has also pressed ahead with those parts of Route No. 4 of the national network – the 'Celtic Trail' between London and Fishguard – which pass through its area. One length of this route runs from Newport through Caerphilly and Penrhos cutting to join the Taff Trail at Nantgarw. Fortunately, a proposal made in 1990 to utilise this cutting for landfill was not taken forward and in 1997 its use for the Trail was approved by Rhondda Cynon Taff County Borough Council.

It is now possible to walk or cycle along much of the route formerly used by coal trains running between Pontypridd and Newport, although in comparison to those increasingly far-off days the ascending gradient of 1 in 200 from Glyntaff will hardly be noticed.

Driver Reg Young and fireman O'Shea on the last day of service at Newport with No. 3714 about to depart with the service to Pontypridd. *D. K. Jones*

Sources and Bibliography

Research for this book has largely been based on primary source material and information contained in contemporary journals. Information from company minute books and reports and from Board of Trade inspections and other documents came from the Public Record Office at Kew. Private and Local Acts, Parliamentary Notices in *The London Gazette*, British Railways, GWR and Bradshaws timetables, and journals such as the *Railway Times*, the *Railway News*, the *Great Western Railway Magazine* and the *Railway Observer* were consulted at Leicester University Library. Contemporary newspapers, including the *Cardiff & Merthyr Guardian*, the *Cardiff Times*, the *South Wales Daily News* and the *Western Mail*, were researched at Cardiff Central Library.

Books consulted included:

The Aberdare Railway, E. R. Mountford and R. W. Kidner, The Oakwood Press, 1995
Barry Docks and Railways, Vol.1, I. W. Prothero, 1995
Caerphilly Works 1901-1964, E. R. Mountford, Roundhouse Books, 1965
Cardiff and the Marquesses of Bute, J. Davies, University of Wales Press, 1981
The Great Western at War 1939-1945, T. Bryan, Patrick Stephens, 1995
Great Western Auto Trailers: Vols.1 and 2, J. Lewis, Wild Swan, 1991and 1995
History of the Great Western Railway, E. T. MacDermot, GWR, 1927
History of the Port of Cardiff, E. L. Chappell, Priory Press, 1939
The Locomotives of the GWR, Part 10, The Railway Correspondence & Travel Society, 1966
Newport Trams, C. Maggs, The Oakwood Press, 1977
Passenger Tramways of Pontypridd, R. Large, The Oakwood Press, 1977
A Register of GWR Absorbed Coaching Stock 1922/23, E. R. Mountford, The Oakwood Press, 1978
The Rhondda Valleys, E. D. Lewis, University College Cardiff Press, 1958
The South Wales Coal Industry 1841-1875, J. H. Morris and L. J. Williams, Cardiff University of Wales Press, 1955
Top Sawyer: A Biography of David Davies of Llandinam, I. Thomas, Longmans, Green & Co., 1938
Tredegar House, Newport Borough Council, 1982

Acknowledgements

I would like to thank all those who have helped with the preparation of this book, and, in particular, John Burleigh, Ray Caston, Tony Cooke, John Dore-Dennis, Eddie Evans, Michael Hale, Cliff Harris, Alan Jarvis, Bob Jones, Bob Marrows, Terry McCarthy, Brian Miller, Tony Miller, the late Iorwerth Prothero, Dick Riley, Stephen Rowson, Alastair Warrington, Ian Wright and many members of the Welsh Railways Research Circle, Historical Model Railway Society and the Railway & Canal Historical Society, too numerous to mention.

The maps on pages 40 and 55 are © National Library of Scotland and licenced under the Creative Commons (CC-BY) licence to view the licence visit https://creativecommons.org/licenses/by/4.0/

INDEX

Accidents, 134, 137, 140, 142, 144, 147
Alexandra Dock, 4, 6, 7, 29, 41, 52, 68, 70, 84, 85, 97; Dock Co., 19, 33, 37, 38; GWR Docks Department, 89; named for Princess Alexandra, 16; National Box Repair Factory, 87
Alexandra Docks and Railway, 45, 52, 69, 71, 72, 135/136; amalgamation with GWR, 88, 89; amalgamation with PC&NR, 72, 75, 109; attempt to change name, 83; Barnum & Bailey coaches, 145, 146; engine sheds, 131-132; mineral traffic, 82/83, 141-143; motor buses, 82; passenger services, 138-141;proposed new lines, 84; working arrangements with Taff Vale, 74, 82

Barry Dock and Railways, 30, 43, 44, 45, 67, 68, 84, 117
Barry docks, 29, 42, 68, 97
Bassaleg, 5, 50, 127/128; PC&NR sidings, 48
Bassaleg Alexandra Docks line, 71, 73, 84, 93, 97, 127-131
Board of Trade inspection, 21, 46, 47, 53, 56, 57/58, 62, 64/65, 73, 77, 78/79, 83, 101, 106, 107, 109, 112, 116/117, 122
Brecon and Merthyr Railway, 4, 10, 12, 15, 16, 20, 21, 25, 31, 32, 36, 42, 47, 54, 56, 58, 84, 99, 127
Bute Dock, 11, 12, 14, 29, 67

Caerphilly, 5, 10, 12, 45, 58, 70, 121, 148; new station, 122; temporary station, 21
Caerphilly Mountain, 5, 14
Caerphilly-Machen branch see also Machen Loop, 4, 23, 31, 46, 58, 60, 63, 64, 99, 123-127; passenger services, 21, 22, 96
Cardiff, 6, 11
Cardiff Railway, 45, 81, 84, 114; passenger services end, 92
Coal; famine 1873, 29; rates, 33, 39, 41, 57, 67; traffic, 6, 11, 14, 20, 27, 33, 70, 83, 91, 93, 97, 99, 119, 123, 141

Davies, David, 30, 33, 42
Dr Griffith's Tramroad, 40, 78
Dynea, 97, 114

Elliot, (Sir) George, 16, 17, 19, 25, 30, 31, 33, 36, 37, 44, 45, 46, 49, 53, 54, 60, 62, 63, 68, 69; death, 69, 72
Excursion trains, 22, 99, 154

First World War, 6, 84, 85, 147/148
Fountain Bridge, 81, 125

Glyntaff, 41, 75, 92, 107, 156, 157; extensions from, 32, 39, 43, 71
Great Western Railway, 4, 9, 16, 27, 32, 39, 41, 43, 51, 68, 84, 114; sale of PC&NR, 69; stops PC&NR trains, 47/48, 49; runs PC&NR services, 74, 75, 87, 140
Groeswen, 76, 97, 115
Grouping, 88, 133, 149

Henshaw, Alfred, 49, 56, 60, 61, 69, 71, 73, 107, 140

Interchange sidings, 61/62, 83, 105, 134, 136, 157

London and North Western Railway, 9, 27, 32, 41, 84

Machen, 5, 10, 20, 94, 125, 127, 148
Machen Loop, 32, 36, 62-67, 125; adverse gradient, 31, 62, 125, 133; BoT inspection, 64, 65; transfer to B&MR, 65
Marquess of Bute, 11, 29, 36, 67
Mendalgief sidings, 56, 62, 83
Monmouthshire Canal, 6, 7, 51
Morgan III, Charles, 1st Baron Tredegar, 15, 19
Morgan, Godfrey, 2nd Baron Tredegar, 19, 38, 43, 50-55, 68, 73; pursuit of unpaid PC&NR tolls, 56
Motor buses, 82, 91/92, 94, 95

Nantgarw, 45, 75, 89, 92, 97, 117
Nationalisation, 93, 153
Newbridge see Pontypridd, 11
Newport, 6, 7, 37, 70, 148; Dock Street station, 9; High Street station, 9; Town (Old) Dock, 14
Nine Mile Point, 7, 10, 84
Nixon's Private Railway, 43/44

Ogmore Dock and Railway, 43, 44, 67

Passenger service decline, 91, 94, 96, 125
Penarth North Curve, 32, 33, 39, 99
Penrhos Caerphilly line, 21, 23, 41, 62, 66, 104-123
Penrhos Junction, 12, 25, 41, 58, 84, 117
Penrhos Walnut Tree Junction, 23, 117, 119, 120
Pontypridd, 6, 11, 23, 31, 40, 41, 81, 101; station, 60, 62, 70, 72, 78, 89, 103
Pontypridd Penrhos line, 40, 41, 60, 64, 99; end of passenger services, 96
Pontypridd, Caerphilly & Newport Railway; Bill, 32;amalgamation with AD&R, 72, 75, 109; BoT inspection, 57-58; extensions, 40,

43/44; GWR stops trains, 47/48, 49; intermediate stations, 61, 107; official opening, 47; Pontypridd station, 60; proposed sale to GWR, 69; traffic, 69; unpaid tolls for TPMR, 56/57; working arrangements with B&MR, 64, 133; working arrangements with Taff Vale, 45, 71, 74, 82, 133; junction with Taff Vale Railway, 46, 101
Powell Druffryn Steam Coal Co., 17, 25, 27, 30, 43, 47, 70, 136

Rail motors, 75-81, 109, 143, 146; B&MR, 80; Cardiff Railway, 81; GWR, 80, 87; purchase, 77, 78; Rhymney Railway, 81, 144
Rhondda coalfield, 29, 42, 90, 97; PC&NR extension, 40
Rhydyfelin, 76, 80, 89, 92, 94, 114
Rhymney Railway, 4, 10, 11, 12, 20, 21, 23, 25, 31, 32, 36, 44, 45, 61, 66/67, 71, 78, 84, 117, 118, 122, 147; proposed lines from PC&NR, 38/39

Second World War, 93, 149, 153
Sirhowy Tramway, 6, 7, 9, 15
South Wales main line, 20, 32, 94, 99, 130; conversion to standard gauge, 21
South Wales Railway, 6, 9
Swansea, 6, 15, 97

Taff Vale Ironworks, 25, 32, 40
Taff Vale Railway, 4, 6, 7, 11, 12, 20, 23, 27, 29, 32, 36, 39, 43, 44, 45, 47, 60, 67, 72, 101; proposed Newport station, 75; running powers over PC&NR lines, 72, 82
Taff Viaduct, 46, 105, 107, 157
Tram Road, 78, 80, 89, 104, 111, 148
Trams, 81-82
Tredegar Park Mile Railway, 4, 7, 32, 42, 43, 50-56, 72, 89, 129; GWR lines, 52, 73; PC&NR line opens, 56; purchased by GWR, 90
Treforest, 45, 92, 97, 108, 111

Upper Boat, 92, 97, 115

Van, 12, 20, 32, 64

Walnut Tree Bridge (Junction), 11, 12, 75, 99
Waterloo, 81, 125
Western Valleys Junction, 20
Western Valleys Line, 9, 20, 32, 42, 73, 84, 129
White Hart, 81